# J. R. R. Tolkien

is today the most widely read and discussed author on college campuses in America. *The Hobbit* and his famous trilogy, "The Lord of the Rings," have been acclaimed as masterpieces of fantasy, unique among the imaginative works of our time.

In this collection are three complete books—*Tree and Leaf, Farmer Giles of Ham,* and *Tom Bombadil,* together with an original play by Tolkien and a marvelously evocative commentary on Tolkien's world of fantasy by Peter S. Beagle.

For anyone who has yet to read *The Hobbit* or "The Lord of the Rings" here is a brilliant introduction to the most captivating author now writing—and for Tolkien fans it is an indispensable addition to the small shelf of books by J. R. R. Tolkien, a book to read, to enjoy, and to keep.

THE AUTHORIZED EDITIONS
*of the works of J. R. R. Tolkien*

THE HOBBIT

*The Lord of the Rings Trilogy*

*Part I*
THE FELLOWSHIP OF THE RING

*Part II*
THE TWO TOWERS

*Part III*
THE RETURN OF THE KING

THE TOLKIEN READER
SMITH OF WOOTON MAJOR
AND FARMER GILES OF HAM

J. R. R. Tolkien was at Pembroke College, Oxford, as Professor of Anglo-Saxon from 1925 to 1945 and then, until his retirement in 1959, as Merton Professor of English Language and Literature. His chief interest was in the literary and linguistic tradition of the English West Midlands, especially in *Beowulf,* the *Ancrene Wisse,* and *Sir Gawain and the Green Knight,* but he is better known to the reading public as the author of *Farmer Giles of Ham, The Hobbit, The Adventures of Tom Bombadil,* and the three volumes of *The Lord of the Rings.*

# THE
# TOLKIEN
# READER

by

## J. R. R. TOLKIEN

BALLANTINE BOOKS • NEW YORK

# CONTENTS

# THE
# TOLKIEN READER

## Publisher's Note

IN compiling a Tolkien Reader, the publishers have felt it wiser not to attempt an anthology of "favorite passages" from *The Hobbit* and *The Lord of the Rings* but to present, instead, a collection of shorter works by Professor Tolkien which have not previously been available in paperback form.

*Tree and Leaf,* published as a separate book in hardcover by Houghton Mifflin Company, contains Professor Tolkien's famous essay on the form of the fairy story and its particular values of Fantasy, Recovery, Escape and Consolation, followed by the story "Leaf by Niggle" which illustrates the ideas suggested.

*Farmer Giles of Ham,* an imaginative history of the distant and marvelous past, introduces a new hero, the unheroic Farmer Giles, whose efforts to capture a wealthy but somewhat untrustworthy dragon will delight adults as well as children.

*The Adventures of Tom Bombadil* is a collection of verse about the "master of wood, water and hill," ballads in praise of Tom Bombadil (staunch friend of Hobbits and a welcome figure in *The Lord of the Rings.*)

To these established favorites, Professor Tolkien has graciously permitted the publishers to add "The Homecoming of Beorhtnoth Beorhthelm's Son," a short play based on *The Battle of Malden*, a fragment of an epic poem describing an actual battle fought in the tenth century between the Viking invaders and the English commanded by Beorhtnoth of Essex. In the following commentary, comparing the original poem to *Beowulf*, the reader may enter the realm of Professor Tolkien's professional studies of early English saga, the inspiration for his own mythic creation of Middle Earth in *The Lord of the Rings*.

For those who have yet to read that epic fantasy trilogy, Peter Beagle's appreciation, "Tolkien's Magic Ring," will serve as the perfect introduction.

# Tolkien's Magic Ring

Three Rings for the Elven-kings under the sky,
Seven for the Dwarf-lords in their halls of stone,
Nine for Mortal Men, doomed to die,
   One for the Dark Lord on his dark throne
In the Land of Mordor where the Shadows lie.
   One Ring to rule them all, One Ring to find them,
   One Ring to bring them all and in the darkness bind them
In the Land of Mordor where the Shadows lie.


Far to the north there are the Iron Hills, the Gray Mountains and the Ice Bay of Forochel; beyond that lies only the great Northern Waste. Farthest to the south is the Haradwaith, land of a dark and fierce people; on the west is the Sea, and far over the Sea are the immortal lands of Westernesse, out of which the Eldar peoples came, and to which they will all return in time. To the east is Mordor, and that was always an evil and desolate country. These are the boundaries of Middle-earth, and this is the world that J. R. R. Tolkien has explored and chronicled in *The Lord of the Rings*. I do not say *created*, for it was always there.

*The Lord of the Rings* and its prologue, *The Hobbit*, belong, in my experience, to a small group of books and poems and songs that I have truly shared with other people. The strangest strangers turn out to know it, and we talk about Gandalf and mad Gollum and the bridge of Khazad-dûm while the party or the classroom or the train rattles along unheard. Old friends rediscover it, as I do—to browse through any book of the *Ring* trilogy is to get hooked once more into the whole legend —and we talk of it at once as though we had just read it for the first time, and as though we were remembering something that had happened to us together long ago. Something of ourselves has gone into reading it, and so it belongs to us.

The country of the book, Middle-earth, is a land much like our own, as mythical, but no more so. Its sunlight is remembered from the long summers of childhood, and its nightmares are equally those of children: overwhelming visions of great, cold shapes that block out the sunlight forever. But the forces that form the lives of the dwellers in Middle-earth are the same that make our lives—history, chance and desire. It is a world bubbling with possibility, subject to natural law, and never more than a skin away from the howling primal chaos that waits outside every world; it is no Oz, no Great Good Place, but a world inhabited by people and things, smells and seasons, like our own.

*The Hobbit* is our introduction both to Middle-earth and to the tale of the One Ring. Hobbits are a small, burrow-dwelling people, a little shorter than Dwarves: furry-footed, sociable growers and gardeners, fond of fireworks, songs and tobacco, inclined toward stoutness and the drawing up of genealogies. In this book, the hobbit Bilbo Baggins accompanies thirteen Dwarves and a wizard named Gandalf to aid in the recovery of a treasure stolen by a dragon centuries before. During the adventure Bilbo finds a magic ring and brings it home as a souvenir. Its gift, as far as he can tell, is to make the wearer invisible, which is useful if you are trying to avoid aunts and dragons, and Bilbo uses it for both purposes a time or two. But he makes little other use of it in the sixty years he keeps it; he carries it in his pocket on a fine chain.

*The Lord of the Rings* begins with Gandalf's discovery that Bilbo's ring is in truth the One Ring of the rhyme. It was made by the Dark Lord—Sauron of Mordor, ageless and utterly evil—and the lesser rings distributed among Elves, Dwarves and Men are meant in time to lure the three peoples under the domination of the One Ring, the master of all. But Sauron has lost the ring, and his search for it is growing steadily more fierce and frantic: possessing the Ring, he would be finally invincible, but without it all his power may yet be unmade. The Ring must be destroyed—not only to keep it from Sauron's grasp, but because of all the rings, the One Ring's nature is to turn good into evil—and it is Bilbo's nephew, Frodo Baggins, who undertakes to journey with it to the volcano where it was forged, even though the mountain lies in Mordor, under the eye of the Dark Lord.

*The Lord of the Rings* is the tale of Frodo's journey through a long nightmare of greed and terrible energy, of his education in both fear and true beauty, and of his final loss of the world he seeks to save. In a sense, his growing knowledge has eaten up the joy and the innocent strength that made him, of all the wise and magic people he encounters, the only one fit to bear the Ring. As he tells Sam Gamgee, the only friend who followed him all the long way to the fire, "It must often be so . . . when things are in danger: someone has to give them up, lose them, so that others may keep them." There are others in Middle-earth who would have willingly paid that price, but certainly none to whom it would have meant as much.

That is the plot; but the true delight of the book comes from the richness of the epic, of which *The Lord of the Rings* is only a few stanzas. The structure of Tolkien's world is as dizzyingly complex and as natural as a snowflake or a spiderweb: the kingdoms of Men in Middle-earth alone have endured for three ages, and each of their histories, as Tolkien sets them forth in the fascinating Appendix, contains enough material for a ballad as long as *The Lord of the Rings*. And there are other, older peoples—notably the immortal Elves—whose memories go back to the Elder Days, long before good or evil moved in Middle-earth; there are the Dwarves and the Ents—the shepherds of the trees, "old as mountains"—and there is Tom Bombadil, who belongs to no race, no mission and no age.

Tolkien tells us something of each of these peoples—their songs, their languages, their legends, their customs and their relations with one another—but he is wise enough not to tell all that he knows of them and of their world. One can do that with literary creations, but not with anything living. And Middle-earth lives, not only in *The Lord of the Rings* but around it and back and forth from it. I have read the complete work five or six times (not counting browsing, for which this essay is, in part, an excuse), and each time my pleasure in the texture of it deepens. It will bear the mind's handling, and it is a book that acquires an individual patina in each mind that takes it up, like a much-caressed pocket stone or piece of wood. At times, always knowing that I didn't write it, I feel that I did.

*The Hobbit* is a good introduction to the dwellers in Middle-earth, the more so as several of its main characters appear again in *The Lord of the Rings*. In addition to hobbits, Dwarves, Elves and Men, there is Gandalf the wizard: a wanderer, known by many names to many peoples, capable of appearing as a bent, frail old man, handy with fireworks, vain, fussy and somehow comical, or as a shining figure of terrifying power, fit to contest the will of Sauron himself. And there is Beorn, the skin-changer, who can take on the shape of a bear at will; a surly, rumbling man, but a good friend. Beorn is not seen after *The Hobbit,* but in a literary sense he is the forerunner of the more deeply realized Tom Bombadil. Both are wary creatures, mis-liking the great concerns of other peoples. Both are their own masters, under no enchantment but their own; but old Bombadil is song incarnate, and his power is greater than Beorn's. He would be the last to be conquered if Sauron held the Ring.

But of all the characters in both books, surely the most memorable—and by his own miserable fate, the most important—is the creature called Sméagol, or Gollum, from the continuous gulping sound he makes in his throat. Gollum in ancestry is very close to the hobbits, and it is he who discovers the Ring in a river where it has been lost for thousands of years. Rather, he murders to get it, for no reason that he can say except that it is more beautiful than anything that has ever come into his life. His name for it, always, is "the Precious." He flees up the river with it until the river flows under the mountains, and there he hides in darkness until Bilbo, lost in the mountains, stumbles on him and on the unguarded Ring, which he pockets. The Ring takes care of itself, as Gandalf realizes: it gravitates to power;

it goes where it has to go. But Gollum cannot live without his Precious, and it is not long before he leaves the mountains to search for it. In his wanderings, he eventually picks up the trail of Frodo and Sam, and is captured by them and made to lead them into Mordor, where he has once been Sauron's prisoner. From then on he is either along with them or in sight of them almost continuously until the end of their journey—and of his own equally terrible odyssey.

At the time Frodo takes him, Gollum is, of course, quite mad. The dark, silent centuries of living with the Ring's hunger, and the torments of Sauron after that, have burned his mind away to a single, glowing cinder of meaningless desire. He is two creatures now, two voices that hiss and chatter in him night and day: Gollum and Sméagol—one no person at all, no *I,* but the Ring's thing; the other somehow still alive, still retaining a few shreds of its own will after all this long time, and even able to feel a stunted, grotesque yearning toward Frodo, whom he must betray. He cannot abide light—even the face of the moon is a physical anguish to him—and he is afraid of almost everything in the world, most of all Sauron. Moreover, Gollum is dangerous; he has long been a cannibal, and his ruined body keeps a rubbery, unnatural strength. Bilbo and Sam and many others have chances to kill him, but each time the idea of his suffering, vaguely as they may conceive it (and it takes someone who has borne the Ring, even for a little while, to understand Gollum's agony), prevents them; and so he lives to play out his part in the story of the Ring. In the end he haunts the imagination perhaps more than any other character in *The Lord of the Rings,* which is fitting, for he was already a ghost when the story began.

Sauron himself is never seen, except for one terrifying moment when a hobbit's mind makes contact with his in a *palantír,* a seeing-stone.

But Sauron's servants are as visible as their single-minded energy can make them: Orcs and trolls, bred up by him in mockery of Elves and Ents, as incapable of any creation as their lord, taking no delight but in ugliness; barrow-wights, cold spirits dwelling in the ruined burial mounds of kings; all manner of Men, from barbarians of the woods to the cruel Haradrim, who ride "oliphants," to kings and princes who have fallen into Sauron's various traps of means and ends. Of these latter, the most ill-fated, the most lost and ghastly, are the Nazgûl, the Ringwraiths, each of whom was once a man, a king who came under the power of the Nine Rings that were made for mortal men. Astride great birds or riding black horses they cast freezing shadows as they hunt to and fro over Middle-earth on their master's errands, forever calling to one another in thin voices full of evil and a kind of pitiless sorrow. They are creatures out of a child's dream of clouds across the moon, searching for him, called by the beating of his heart; but they are also men destroyed, and Frodo, seeing them with the Ring on his finger, comprehends the nature of their damnation. Their doom is very nearly his.

For the Ring devours. It is a kind of burning glass through which all the selfishness in the world can be brought to focus, and to wear it is to be naked both to the Eye (for Sauron let a great deal of his original strength go into the making of the Ring, and it calls to him) and to one s own deepest desires for power over others. Like everything else that belongs to the Dark Lord, the Ring cannot truly create: it can give power, but only according to the wearer's true strength and stature; and its possessor does not die, "but he does not grow or obtain more life," as Gandalf says, "he merely continues." It has stretched Bilbo's life dangerously thin, and Gollum's past his mind's endurance; and the long burden of it has wounded Frodo beyond healing. He speaks for the wretched Gollum and even for the Nazgûl when he says to Sam:

> No taste of food, no feel of water, no sound of wind, no memory of tree or grass or flower, no image of moon or star are left to me. I am naked in the dark, Sam, and there is no veil between me and the wheel of fire. I begin to see it even with my waking eyes, and all else fades.

The book is full of singing. Ballads and poetry and rhymes of lore belong to the daily lives of the peoples of Middle-earth, and epic poetry is their history and their journalism. Each of the different races and tribes, excepting the dwellers in Mordor, has its own traditions of song, and Tolkien renders them all— from the Elvish modes and patterns of rhyming to the proud

chanting of Dwarves and the music-hall turns that hobbits love
—with the skill and naturalness of a writer whose own prose
is itself taut with poetry. The best of the verses begin to sing
themselves as you read them; as do the names of people and
places, for that matter—one could almost sing the maps that
Tolkien includes with each volume. And the music is never
imposed from outside; it springs from the center of this world,
as it does from the world of the *Iliad* and the *Nibelungenlied*.
Tolkien's people would sing, and they would sing like this.

The books have sold quietly but steadily in the United States
since Houghton Mifflin introduced them, but within the last
few years the sales have begun to gather momentum. Ballantine
Books has published a paperbound version approved by Tolkien,
which includes a foreword and some new material.

The real surge of interest in Tolkien's writing has been
among high school and college students. Students make strange
and varied works their own, and if there is any significance to
their adoption of *The Lord of the Rings*—beyond the fact
that it's a good book—the hell with it; one or another of our
explainers of the young will take note of it pretty soon. But
there is one possible reason for Tolkien's popularity that I
would like to put forward, because it concerns the real strength
of *The Lord of the Rings*. Young people in general sense the
difference between the real and the phony. They don't know it—
when they begin to know that difference, and to try to articulate
it, then they are adults and subject to all the pains and fallibili-
ties of that state. They can be misled by fools or madmen, but
they sense the preacher who doesn't feel a word of his sermon,
the mountebank who is putting them on, the society that does
not believe in itself. They rarely take a phony of any sort to their
hearts.

Tolkien believes in his world, and in all those who inhabit
it. This is, of course, no guarantee of greatness—if Tolkien
weren't a fine writer, it could not make him one—but it is something without which there is no greatness, in art or in anything else, and I find very little of it in the fiction that purports
to tell me about this world we all live in. This failure of belief
on the authors' part is, I think, what turns so many books that
mean to deal with the real things that really happen to the
real souls and bodies of real people in the real world into the

cramped little stages where varyingly fashionable marionettes jiggle and sing. But I believe that Tolkien has wandered in Middle-earth, which exists nowhere but in himself, and I understand the sadness of the Elves, and I have seen Mordor.

And this is the source of the book's unity, this deep sureness of Tolkien's that makes his world more than the sum of all its parts, more than an ingenious contrivance, more than an easy parable of power. Beyond the skill and invention of the man, beyond his knowledge of philology, mythology and poetry, *The Lord of the Rings* is made with love and pride and a little madness. There never has been much fiction of any sort made in this manner, but on some midnights it does seem to me that my time is cheating itself of even this little. So I have read the tale of the Ring and some other books many times, and I envy my children, who have not yet read any of them, and I envy you if you have not, and wish you joy.

PETER S. BEAGLE

PETER S. BEAGLE was born in New York in 1939 and wrote his first novel, *A Fine and Private Place,* before he was twenty. It was published in 1960, and was extremely well received.

After graduation from the University of Pittsburgh in 1959, Mr. Beagle went abroad, where he lived in Paris and traveled in France, Italy and England. He spent a year at Stanford University on a Writing Fellowship, and now lives in Santa Cruz, California. His stories have appeared in *Seventeen* and *The Atlantic Monthly,* and he has contributed articles to *Holiday,* where portions of his second novel, *I See by My Outfit,* were published.

# THE
# HOMECOMING
# OF
# BEORHTNOTH
# BEORHTHELM'S SON

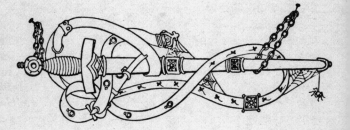

# THE HOMECOMING of BEORHTNOTH BEORHTHELM'S SON

*by* J. R. R. TOLKIEN

# I

## BEORHTNOTH'S DEATH

In August of the year 991, in the reign of Æthelred II, a battle was fought near Maldon in Essex. On the one side was the defence-force of Essex, on the other a viking host that had ravaged Ipswich. The English were commanded by Beorhtnoth son of Beorhthelm, the duke of Essex, a man renowned in his day: powerful, fearless, proud. He was now old and hoar, but vigorous and valiant, and his white head towered high above other men, for he was exceedingly tall,[1] The "Danes"—they were on this occasion probably for the most part Norwegians— were, according to one version of the Anglo-Saxon Chronicle, led by Anlaf, famous in Norse saga and history as Olaf Tryggvason, later to become King of Norway.[2] The Northmen had sailed up the estuary of the Pante, now called the Blackwater, and encamped on Northey Island. The Northmen and the English were thus separated by an arm of the river; filled by the incoming tide, it could only be crossed by a "bridge" or causeway, difficult to force in the face of a determined defence.[3] The defence was resolute. But the vikings knew, or so it would seem, what manner of a man they had to deal with: they asked

---

[1] According to one estimate 6 foot 9 inches tall. This estimate was based on the length and size of his bones when examined, in his tomb at Ely, in A.D. 1769.

[2] That Olaf Tryggvason was actually present at Maldon is now thought to be doubtful. But his name was known to Englishmen. He had been in Britain before, and was certainly here again in 994.

[3] According to the views of E. D. Laborde, now generally accepted. The causeway or "hard" between Northey and the mainland is still there.

for leave to cross the ford, so that a fair fight could be joined. Beorhtnoth accepted the challenge and allowed them to cross. This act of pride and misplaced chivalry proved fatal. Beorhtnoth was slain and the English routed; but the duke's "household", his *heorðwerod*, containing the picked knights and officers of his bodyguard, some of them members of his own family, fought on, until they all fell dead beside their lord.

A fragment—a large fragment, 325 lines long—of a contemporary poem has been preserved: it has no end and no beginning, and no title, but is now generally known as *The Battle of Maldon*. It tells of the demand of the vikings for tribute in return for peace; of Beorhtnoth's proud refusal, and challenge, and the defence of the "bridge"; the cunning request of the vikings, and the crossing of the causeway; the last fight of Beorhtnoth, the falling of his golden-hilted sword from his maimed hand, and the hewing of his body by the heathen men. The end of the fragment, almost half of it, tells of the last stand of the bodyguard. The names, deeds, and speeches of many of the Englishmen are recorded.

The duke Beorhtnoth was a defender of the monks, and a patron of the church, especially of the abbey of Ely. After the battle the Abbot of Ely obtained his body and buried it in the abbey. His head had been hacked off and was not recovered; it was replaced in the tomb by a ball of wax.

According to the late, and largely unhistorical, account in the twelfth-century *Liber Eliensis* the Abbot of Ely went himself with some of his monks to the battlefield. But in the following poem it is supposed that the abbot and his monks came only as far as Maldon, and that they there remained, sending two men, servants of the duke, to the battlefield some distance away, late in the day after the battle. They took a waggon, and were to bring back Beorhtnoth's body. They left the waggon near the end of the causeway and began to search among the slain: very many had fallen on both sides. Torhthelm (colloquially Totta) is a youth, son of a minstrel; his head is full of old lays concerning the heroes of northern antiquity, such as Finn, King of Frisia; Fróda of the Hathobards; Béowulf; and Hengest and Horsa, traditional leaders of the English Vikings in the days of Vortigern (called by the English Wyrtgeorn). Tídwald (in short Tída) was an old *ceorl*, a farmer

4

who had seen much fighting in the English defence-levies. Neither of these men were actually in the battle. After leaving the waggon they became separated in the gathering dusk. Night falls, dark and clouded. Torhthelm is found alone in a part of the field where the dead lie thick.

From the old poem are derived the proud words of Offa at a council before the battle, and the name of the gallant young Aelfwine (scion of an ancient noble house in Mercia) whose courage was commended by Offa. There also are found the names of the two Wulfmaers: Wulfmaer, son of Beorhtnoth's sister; and Wulfmaer the young, son of Wulfstan, who together with Aelfnoth fell grievously hewn beside Beorhtnoth. Near the end of the surviving fragment an old retainer, Beorhtwold, as he prepares to die in the last desperate stand, utters the famous words, a summing up of the heroic code, that are here spoken in a dream by Torhthelm:

> *Hige sceal þe heardra, heorte þe cenre,*
> *mod sceal þe mare þe ure maegen lytlað.*

"Will shall be the sterner, heart the bolder, spirit the greater as our strength lessens."

It is here implied, as is indeed probable, that these words were not "original," but an ancient and honoured expression of heroic will; Beorhtwold is all the more, not the less, likely for that reason actually to have used them in his last hour.

The third English voice in the dark, speaking after the *Dirige* is first heard, uses rhyme: presaging the fading end of the old heroic alliterative measure. The old poem is composed in a free form of the alliterative line, the last surviving fragment of ancient English heroic minstrelsy. In that measure, little if at all freer (though used for dialogue) than the verse of *The Battle of Maldon*, the present modern poem is written.

The rhyming lines are an echo of some verses, preserved in the *Historia Eliensis*, referring to King Canute:

> Merie sungen ðe muneches binnen Ely,
> oa Cnut ching reu ðerby.
> 'Roweð, cnites, noer the land
> and here we ther muneches saeng'.

# THE HOMECOMING OF BEORHTNOTH
## BEORHTHELM'S SON

*The sound is heard of a man moving uncertainly and breathing
noisily in the darkness. Suddenly a voice speaks,
loudly and sharply.*

TORHTHELM.    Halt! What do you want? Hell take you! Speak!

TÍDWALD.       Totta! I know you by your teeth rattling.

TOR.  Why, Tída, you! The time seemed long
alone among the lost. They lie so queer.
I've watched and waited, till the wind sighing
was like words whispered by waking ghosts
that in my ears muttered.

TÍD.              And your eyes fancied
barrow-wights and bogies. It's a black darkness
since the moon foundered; but mark my words:
not far from here we'll find the master,
by all accounts.

*Tídwald lets out a faint beam from a dark-lantern. An owl
hoots. A dark shape flits through the beam of light. Torhthelm
starts back and overturns the lantern, which Tída had set on
the ground.*

                 What ails you now?

TOR.  Lord save us! Listen!

TÍD.             My lad, you're crazed.
Your fancies and your fears make foes of nothing.
Help me to heave 'em! It's heavy labour to lug them
alone: long ones and short ones, the thick and the
thin. Think less, and talk less of ghosts. Forget your
gleeman's stuff!

Their ghosts are under ground, or else God has them;
and wolves don't walk as in Woden's days,
not here in Essex. If any there be,
they'll be two-leggèd. There, turn him over!
*An owl hoots again.*
It's only an owl.

TOR.                    An ill boding.
Owls are omens. But I'm not afraid,
not of fancied fears. A fool call me,
but more men than I find the mirk gruesome
among the dead unshrouded. It's like the dim shadow
of heathen hell, in the hopeless kingdom
where search is vain. We might seek for ever
and yet miss the master in this mirk, Tída.
    O lord beloved, where do you lie tonight,
your head so hoar upon a hard pillow,
and your limbs lying in long slumber?
*Tídwald lets out again the light of the dark-lantern.*

TÍD.    Look here, my lad, where they lie thickest!
Here! Lend a hand! This head we know!
Wulfmær it is. I'll wager aught
not far did he fall from friend and master.

TOR.    His sister-son! The songs tell us,
ever near shall be at need nephew to uncle.

TÍD.    Nay, he's not here—or he's hewn out of ken.
It was the other I meant, th' Eastsaxon lad,
Wulfstan's youngster. It's a wicked business
to gather them ungrown. A gallant boy, too,
and the makings of a man.

TOR.                    Have mercy on us!
He was younger than I, by a year or more.

TÍD.    Here's Ælfnoth, too, by his arm lying.

TOR.    As he would have wished it. In work or play
they were fast fellows, and faithful to their
lord, as close to him as kin.

7

TÍD.                    Curse this lamplight
        and my eyes' dimness! My oath I'll take
        they fell in his defence, and not far away
        now master lies. Move them gently!

TOR.    Brave lads! But it's bad when bearded men
        put shield at back and shun battle,
        running like roe-deer, while the red heathen
        beat down their boys. May the blast of Heaven
        light on the dastards that to death left them
        to England's shame! And here's Ælfwine:
        barely bearded, and his battle's over.

TÍD.    That's bad, Totta. He was a brave lordling,
        and we need his like: a new weapon
        of the old metal. As eager as fire,
        and as staunch as steel. Stern-tongued at times,
        and outspoken after Offa's sort.

TOR.    Offa! He's silenced. Not all liked him;
        many would have muzzled him, had master let them.
        "There are cravens at council that crow proudly
        with the hearts of hens": so I hear he said
        at the lord's meeting. As lays remind us:
        "What at the mead man vows, when morning comes
        let him with deeds answer, or his drink vomit
        and a sot be shown." But the songs wither,
        and the world worsens. I wish I'd been here,
        not left with the luggage and the lazy thralls,
        cooks and sutlers! By the Cross, Tída,
        I loved him no less than any lord with him;
        and a poor freeman may prove in the end
        more tough when tested than titled earls
        who count back their kin to kings ere Woden.

TÍD.    You can talk, Totta! Your time'll come,
        and it'll look less easy than lays make it.
        Bitter taste has iron, and the bite of swords
        is cruel and cold, when you come to it.
        Then God guard you, if your glees falter!
        When your shield is shivered, between shame

and death is hard choosing. Help me with this
one! There, heave him over—the hound's carcase,
hulking heathen!

Tor.                                 Hide it, Tída!
Put the lantern out! He's looking at me.
I can't abide his eyes, bleak and evil
as Grendel's in the moon.

Tíd.                          Ay, he's a grim fellow,
but he's dead and done-for. Danes don't trouble me
save with swords and axes. They can smile or glare,
once hell has them. Come, haul the next!

Tor. Look! Here's a limb! A long yard, and thick
as three men's thighs.

Tíd.                       I thought as much.
Now bow your head, and hold your babble
for a moment Totta! It's the master at last.
   *There is silence for a short while.*
Well, here he is—or what Heaven's left us:
the longest legs in the land, I guess.

Tor. (*His voice rises to a chant.*)
His head was higher than the helm of kings
with heathen crowns, his heart keener
and his soul clearer than swords of heroes
polished and proven: than plated gold
his worth was greater. From the world has
passed a prince peerless in peace and war,
just in judgment, generous-handed
as the golden lords of long ago.
He has gone to God glory seeking,
Beorhtnoth beloved.

Tíd.                     Brave words my lad!
The woven stars have yet worth in them
for woeful hearts. But there's work to do,
ere the funeral begins.

TOR.                            I've found it, Tída!
Here's his sword lying! I could swear to it
by the golden hilts.

TÍD.                            I'm glad to hear it,
How it was missed is a marvel. He is marred cruelly.
Few tokens else shall we find on him;
they've left us little of the Lord we knew.

TOR.    Ah, woe and worse! The wolvish heathens
have hewn off his head, and the hulk left us
mangled with axes. What a murder it is,
this bloody fighting!

TÍD.                            Aye, that's the battle for you,
and no worse today than wars you sing of,
when Fróda fell, and Finn was slain.
The world wept then, as it weeps today:
you can hear the tears through the harp's
twanging. Come, bend your back. We must bear away
the cold leavings. Catch hold of the legs!
Now lift—gently! Now lift again!
        *They shuffle along slowly.*

TOR.    Dear still shall be this dead body,
        though men have marred it.
    *Torhthelm's voice rises again to a chant.*
                            Now mourn for ever
Saxon and English, from the sea's margin
to the western forest! The wall is fallen,
women are weeping; the wood is blazing
and the fire flaming as a far beacon.
Build high the barrow his bones to keep!
For here shall be hid both helm and sword;
and to the ground be given golden corslet,
and rich raiment and rings gleaming,
wealth unbegrudged for the well-beloved;
of the friends of men first and noblest,
to his hearth-comrades help unfailing,
to his folk the fairest father of peoples.

Glory loved he; now glory earning
his grave shall be green, while ground or sea,
while word or woe in the world lasteth.

TÍD. Good words enough, gleeman Totta!
You laboured long as you lay, I guess,
in the watches of the night, while the wise slumbered.
But I'd rather have rest, and my rueful thoughts.
These are Christian days, though the cross is heavy;
Beorhtnoth we bear not Béowulf here:
no pyres for him, nor piling of mounds;
and the gold will be given to the good abbot.
Let the monks mourn him and mass be chanted!
With learned Latin they'll lead him home,
if we can bring him back. The body's weighty!

TOR. Dead men drag earthward. Now down a spell!
My back's broken, and the breath has left me.

TÍD. If you spent less in speech, you would speed better.
But the cart's not far, so keep at it!
Now start again, and in step with me!
A steady pace does it.
    *Torhthelm halts suddenly.*
        You stumbling dolt,
Look where you're going!

TOR.                 For the Lord's pity,
halt, Tída, here! Hark now, and look!

TÍD. Look where, my lad?

TOR.              To the left yonder.
There's a shade creeping, a shadow darker
than the western sky, there walking crouched!
Two now together! Troll-shapes, I guess,
or hell-walkers. They've a halting gait,
groping groundwards with grisly arms.

TÍD. Nameless nightshades—naught else can I see,
till they walk nearer. You're witch-sighted
to tell fiends from men in this foul darkness.

11

TOR. Then listen, Tída! There are low voices,
moans and muttering, and mumbled laughter.
They are moving hither!

TÍD.                     Yes, I mark it now,
I can hear something.

TOR.                     Hide the lantern!

TÍD. Lay down the body and lie by it!
Now stone-silent! There are steps coming.
*They crouch on the ground. The sound of stealthy steps
grows louder and nearer. When they are close at hand
            Tídwald suddenly shouts out:*
Hullo there, my lads! You're late comers,
if it's fighting you look for; but I can find
you some, if you need it tonight.
You'll get nothing cheaper.

*There is a noise of scuffling in the dark. Then there is a
shriek. Torhthelm's voice rings out shrill.*

TOR. You snuffling swine, I'll slit you for it!
Take your trove then! Ho! Tída there!
I've slain this one. He'll slink no more.
If swords he was seeking, he soon found one,
by the biting end.

TÍD.                My bogey-slayer!
Bold heart would you borrow with
Beorhtnoth's sword?
Nay, wipe it clean! And keep your wits!
That blade was made for better uses.
You wanted no weapon: a wallop on the nose,
or a boot behind, and the battle's over
with the likes of these. Their life's wretched,
but why kill the creatures, or crow about it?
There are dead enough around. Were he a Dane, mind you,
I'd let you boast—and there's lots abroad
not far away, the filthy thieves:
I hate 'em, by my heart, heathen or sprinkled,
the Devil's offspring.

TOR.                    The Danes, you say!
Make haste! Let's go! I'd half forgotten.
There may be more at hand our murder plotting.
We'll have the pirate pack come pouring on us,
if they hear us brawling.

TÍD.                    My brave swordsman!
These weren't Northmen! Why should Northmen come?
They've had their fill of hewing and fighting,
and picked their plunder: the place is bare.
They're in Ipswich now with the ale running,
or lying off London in their long vessels,
while they drink to Thor and drown the sorrow
of hell's children. These are hungry folk
and masterless men, miserable skulkers.
They're corpse-strippers: a cursèd game
and shame to think of. What are you shuddering at?

TOR.  Come on now quick! Christ forgive me,
and these evil days, when unregretted
lie mouldering, and the manner of wolves
the folk follow in fear and hunger,
their dead unpitying to drag and plunder!
Look there yonder! There's a lean shadow,
a third of the thieves. Let's thrash the villain!

TÍD.  Nay, let him alone! Or we'll lose the way.
As it is we've wandered, and I'm bewildered enough.
He won't try attacking two men by himself.
Lift your end there! Lift up, I say.
Put your foot forward.

TOR.                    Can you find it, Tída?
I haven't a notion now in these nightshadows
where we left the waggon. I wish we were back!
*They shuffle along without speaking for a while.*
Walk wary, man! There's water by us;
you'll blunder over the brink. Here's the Blackwater!

13

Another step that way, and in the stream
we'd be like fools floundering—and the flood's running.

TÍD.    We've come to the causeway. The cart's near it,
so courage, my boy. If we can carry him on
few steps further, the first stage is passed.
               *They move a few paces more.*
By Edmund's head! though his own's missing,
our Lord's not light. Now lay him down!
Here's the waggon waiting. I wish we could drink
his funeral ale without further trouble
on the bank right here. The beer he gave
was good and plenty to gladden your heart,
both strong and brown. I'm in a stew of sweat.
Let's stay a moment.

TOR.    (*After a pause.*)        It's strange to me
how they came across this causeway here,
or forced a passage without fierce battle;
but there are few tokens to tell of fighting.
A hill of heathens one would hope to find,
but none lie near.

TÍD.                    No more's the pity.
Alas, my friend, our lord was at fault,
or so in Maldon this morning men were saying.
Too proud, too princely! But his pride's cheated,
and his princedom has passed, so we'll praise his valour.
He let them cross the causeway, so keen was he
to give minstrels matter for mighty songs.
Needlessly noble. It should never have been:
bidding bows be still, and the bridge opening,
matching more with few in mad handstrokes!
Well, doom he dared, and died for it.

TOR.    So the last is fallen of the line of earls,
from Saxon lords long-descended
who sailed the seas, as songs tell us,
from Angel in the East, with eager swords
upon war's anvil the Welsh smiting.

Realms here they won and royal kingdoms,
and in olden days this isle conquered.
And now from the North need comes again:
wild blows the wind of war to Britain!

TÍD. And in the neck we catch it, and are nipped as chill
as poor men were then. Let the poets babble,
but perish all pirates! When the poor are robbed
and lose the land they loved and toiled on,
they must die and dung it. No dirge for them,
and their wives and children work in serfdom.

TOR. But Æthelred'll prove less easy prey
than Wyrtgeorn was; and I'll wager, too,
this Anlaf of Norway will never equal
Hengest or Horsa!

TÍD.       We'll hope not, lad!
Come, lend your hand to the lifting again,
then your task is done. There, turn him round!
Hold the shanks now, while I heave the shoulders.
Now, up your end! Up! That's finished.
There cover him with the cloth.

TOR.      It should be clean linen
not a dirty blanket.

TÍD.      It must do for now.
The monks are waiting in Maldon for us,
and the abbot with them. We're hours behind.
Get up now and in. Your eyes can weep,
or your mouth can pray. I'll mind the horses.
Gee up, boys, then. (*He cracks a whip.*) Gee up, and away.

TOR. God guide our road to a good ending!
  *There is a pause, in which a rumbling and a creaking of*
      *wheels is heard.*
How these wheels do whine! They'll hear
the creak for miles away over mire and stone.

A longer pause in which no word is spoken.
Where first do we make for? Have we far to go?
The night is passing, and I'm near finished . . .
Say, Tída, Tída! is your tongue stricken?

TÍD.    I'm tired of talk. My tongue's resting.
"Where first" you say? A fool's question!
To Maldon and the monks, and then miles
onward to Ely and the abbey. It'll end sometime;
but the roads are bad in these ruinous days.
No rest for you yet! Were you reckoning on bed?
The best you'll get is the bottom of the cart
with his body for bolster.

TOR.                 You're a brute, Tída.

TÍD.    It's only plain language. If a poet sang you:
"I bowed my head on his breast beloved,
and weary of weeping woeful slept I;
thus joined we journeyed, gentle master
and faithful servant, over fen and boulder
to his last resting and love's ending",
you'd not call it cruel. I have cares of my own
in my heart, Totta, and my head's weary.
I am sorry for you, and for myself also.
Sleep, lad, then! Sleep! The slain won't trouble,
if your head be heavy, or the wheels grumble.
    He speaks to the horses.
Gee up, my boys! And on you go!
There's food ahead and fair stables,
for the monks are kind. Put the miles behind!

The creaking and rattling of the waggon, and the sound of
hoofs, continue for some time, during which no words are
spoken. After a while lights glimmer in the distance.
Torhthelm speaks from the waggon, drowsily and half
dreaming.

TOR.    There are candles in the dark and cold voices.
I hear mass chanted for master's soul
in Ely isle. Thus ages pass,
and men after men. Mourning voices
of women weeping. So the world passes;

day follows day, and the dust gathers,
his tomb crumbles, as time gnaws it,
and his kith and kindred out of ken dwindle.
So men flicker and in the mirk go out.
The world withers and the wind rises;
the candles are quenched. Cold falls the night.

*The lights disappear as he speaks. Torhthelm's voice becomes louder, but it is still the voice of one speaking in a dream.*

It's dark! It's dark, and doom coming!
Is no light left us? A light kindle,
and fan the flame! Lo! Fire now wakens,
hearth is burning, house is lighted,
men there gather. Out of the mists they come
through darkling doors whereat doom waiteth.
Hark! I hear them in the hall chanting:
stern words they sing with strong voices.
(*He chants*) Heart shall be bolder, harder be purpose,
more proud the spirit as our power lessens!
Mind shall not falter nor mood waver,
though doom shall come and dark conquer.

*There is a great bump and jolt of the cart.*

Hey! what a bump, Tída! My bones are shaken,
and my dream shattered. It's dark and cold.

TÍD.    Aye, a bump on the bone is bad for dreams,
and it's cold waking. But your words were queer,
Torhthelm my lad, with your talk of wind
and doom conquering and a dark ending.
It sounded fey and fell-hearted,
and heathenish, too: I don't hold with that.
It's night right enough; but there's no firelight:
dark is over all, and dead is master.
When morning comes, it'll be much like others:
more labour and loss till the land's ruined;
ever work and war till the world passes.

*The cart rumbles and bumps on.*

Hey! rattle and bump over rut and boulder!
The roads are rough and rest is short
for English men in Æthelred's day.

*The rumbling of the cart dies away. There is complete silence for a while. Slowly the sound of voices chanting begins to be heard. Soon the words, though faint, can be distinguished.*

> Dirige, Domine, in conspectu tuo viam meam.
> Introibo in domum tuam: adorabo ad templum
> Sanctum tuum in timore tuo.

(*A Voice in the dark*):    Sadly they sing, the monks of Ely isle!
> Row men, row! Let us listen here
> a while!

*The chanting becomes loud and clear. Monks bearing a bier amid tapers pass across the scene.*

> Dirige, Domine, in conspectu tuo viam meam.
> Introibo in domum tuam: adorabo ad templum
> sanctum tuum in timore tuo.
>
> Domine, deduc me in iustitia tua: propter
> inimicos meos dirige in conspectu tuo viam
> meam.
>
> Gloria Patri et Filio et Spiritui Sancto: sicut
> erat in principio et nunc et semper et in
> saecula saeculorum.
>
> Dirige, Domine, in conspectu tuo viam meam.
> *They pass, and the chanting fades into silence.*

## (III)

## OFERMOD

This piece, somewhat larger than the Old English fragment that inspired it, was composed primarily as verse, to be condemned or approved as such.[1] But to merit a place in *Essays and Studies* it must, I suppose, contain at least by implication criticism of the matter and manner of the Old English poem (or of its critics).

From that point of view it may be said to be an extended comment on lines 89, 90 of the original: *ða se eorl ongan for his ofermode alyfan landes to fela laþere ðeode*, "then the earl in his overmastering pride actually yielded ground to the enemy, as he should not have done". *The Battle of Maldon* has usually been regarded rather as an extended comment on, or illustration of the words of the old retainer Beorhtwold, 312, 313, cited above, and used in the present piece. They are the best-known lines of the poem, possibly of all Old English verse. Yet except in the excellence of their expression, they seem to me of less interest than the earlier lines; at any rate the full force of the poem is missed unless the two passages are considered together.

---

[1] It was indeed plainly intended as a recitation for two persons, two shapes in "dim shadow", with the help of a few gleams of light and appropriate noises and a chant at the end. It has, of course, never been performed.

19

The words of Beorhtwold have been held to be the finest expression of the northern heroic spirit, Norse or English; the clearest statement of the doctrine of uttermost endurance in the service of indomitable will. The poem as a whole has been called "the only purely heroic poem extant in Old English". Yet the doctrine appears in this clarity, and (approximate) purity, precisely because it is put in the mouth of a subordinate, a man for whom the object of his will was decided by another, who had no responsibility downwards, only loyalty upwards. Personal pride was therefore in him at its lowest, and love and loyalty at their highest.

For this "northern heroic spirit" is never quite pure; it is of gold and an alloy. Unalloyed it would direct a man to endure even death unflinching, when necessary: that is when death may help the achievement of some object of will, or when life can only be purchased by denial of what one stands for. But since such conduct is held admirable, the alloy of personal good name was never wholly absent. Thus Leofsunu in *The Battle of Maldon* holds himself to his loyalty by the fear of reproach if he returns home alive. This motive may, of course, hardly go beyond "conscience": self-judgement in the light of the opinion of his peers, to which the "hero" himself wholly assents; he would act the same, if there were no witnesses.[1] Yet this element of pride, in the form of the desire for honour and glory, in life and after death, tends to grow, to become a chief motive, driving a man beyond the bleak heroic necessity to excess—to chivalry. "Excess" certainly, even if it be approved by contemporary opinion, when it not only goes beyond need and duty, but interferes with it.

Thus Beowulf (according to the motives ascribed to him by the student of heroic-chivalric character who wrote the poem about him) does more than he need, eschewing weapons in order to make his struggle with Grendel a "sporting" fight: which will enhance his personal glory; though it will put him in unnecessary peril, and weaken his chances of ridding the Danes of an intolerable affliction. But Beowulf has no duty to the Danes, he is still a subordinate with no responsibilities downwards; and his glory is also the honour of his side, of the

[1] Cf. *Sir Gawain and the Green Knight*, 2127–31.

Geatas; above all, as he himself says, it will redound to the credit of the lord of his allegiance, Hygelac. Yet he does not rid himself of his chivalry, the excess persists, even when he is an old king upon whom all the hopes of a people rest. He will not deign to lead a force against the dragon, as wisdom might direct even a hero to do; for, as he explains in a long "vaunt", his many victories have relieved him of fear. He will only use a sword on this occasion, since wrestling singlehanded with a dragon is too hopeless even for the chivalric spirit. But he dismisses his twelve companions. He is saved from defeat, and the essential object, destruction of the dragon, only achieved by the loyalty of a subordinate. Beowulf's chivalry would otherwise have ended in his own useless death, with the dragon still at large. As it is, a subordinate is placed in greater peril than he need have been, and though he does not pay the penalty of his master's *mod* with his own life, the people lose their king disastrously.

In *Beowulf* we have only a legend of "excess" in a chief. The case of Beorhtnoth is still more pointed even as a story; but it is also drawn from real life by a contemporary author. Here we have Hygelac behaving like young Beowulf: making a "sporting fight" on level terms; but at other people's expense. In his situation he was not a subordinate, but the authority to be obeyed on the spot; and he was responsible for all the men under him, not to throw away their lives except with one object, the defence of the realm from an implacable foe. He says himself that it is his purpose to defend the ream of Æthelred, the people, and the land (52–3). It was heroic for him and his men to fight, to annihilation if necessary, in the attempt to destroy or hold off the invaders. It was wholly unfitting that he should treat a desperate battle with this sole real object as a sporting match, to the ruin of his purpose and duty.

Why did Beorhtnoth do this? Owing to a defect of character, no doubt; but a character, we may surmise, not only formed by nature, but moulded also by "aristocratic tradition", enshrined in tales and verse of poets now lost save for echoes. Beorhtnoth was chivalrous rather than strictly heroic. Honour was in itself a motive, and he sought it at the risk of placing his *heorðwerod*, all the men most dear to him, in a truly heroic situation, which they could redeem only by death. Magnificent perhaps, but certainly wrong. Too foolish to be heroic. And the folly Beorhtnoth at any rate could not wholly redeem by death.

This was recognized by the poet of *The Battle of Maldon*, though the lines in which his opinion are expressed are little regarded, or played down. The translation of them given above is (I believe) accurate in representing the force and implication of his words, though most will be more familiar with Ker's: "then the earl of his overboldness granted ground too much to the hateful people".[1] They are lines in fact of *severe* criticism, though not incompatible with loyalty, and even love. Songs of praise at Beorhtnoth's funeral may well have been made of him, not unlike the lament of the twelve princes for Beowulf; but they too may have ended on the ominous note struck by the last word of the greater poem: *lofgeornost* "most desirous of glory".

So far as the fragment of his work goes, the poet of *Maldon* did not elaborate the point contained in lines 89–90; though if the poem had any rounded ending and final appraisement (as is likely, for it is certainly not a work of hot haste), it was probably resumed. Yet if he felt moved to criticize and express disapproval at all, then his study of the behaviour of the *heorðwerod,* lacks the sharpness and tragic quality that he intended, if his criticism is not fully valued. By it the loyalty of the retinue is greatly enhanced. Their part was to endure and die, and not to question, though a recording poet may fairly comment that someone had blundered. In their situation heroism was superb. Their duty was unimpaired by the error of their master, and (more poignantly) neither in the hearts of those near to the old man was love lessened. It is the heroism of obedience and love not of pride or wilfulness that is the most heroic and the most moving; from Wiglaf under his kinsman's shield, to Beorhtwold at Maldon, down to Balaclava, even if

---

[1] *To fela* means in Old English idiom that no ground at all should have been conceded. And *ofermod* does not mean "overboldness", not even if we give full value to the *ofer,* remembering how strongly the taste and wisdom of the English (whatever their actions) rejected "excess". *Wita scal gepyldig . . . ne næfre gielpes to georn, ær he geare cunne.* But *mod,* though it may contain or imply courage, does not mean "boldness" any more than Middle English *corage.* It means "spirit", or when unqualified "high spirit", of which the most usual manifestation is pride. But in *ofer-mod* it is qualified, with disapproval: *ofermod* is in fact always a word of condemnation. In verse the noun occurs only twice, once applied to Beorhtnoth, and once to Lucifer.

22

it is enshrined in verse no better than *The Charge of the Light Brigade.*

Beorhtnoth was wrong, and he died for his folly. But it was a noble error, or the error of a noble. It was not for his *heorowerod* to blame him; probably many would not have felt him blameworthy, being themselves noble and chivalrous. But poets, as such, are above chivalry, or even heroism; and if they give any depth to their treatment of such themes, then, even in spite of themselves, these "moods" and the objects to which they are directed will be questioned.

We have two poets that study at length the heroic and chivalrous, with both art and thought, in the older ages: one near the beginning in *Beowulf;* one near the end in *Sir Gawain.* And probably a third, more near the middle, in *Maldon,* if we had all his work. It is not surprising that any consideration of the work of one of these leads to the others. *Sir Gawain,* the latest, is the most fully conscious, and is in plain intention a criticism or valuation of a whole code of sentiment and conduct, in which heroic courage is only a part, with different loyalties to serve. Yet it is a poem with many inner likenesses to *Beowulf,* deeper than the use of the old "alliterative"[1] metre, which is none the less significant. Sir Gawain, as the exemplar of chivalry, is of course shown to be deeply concerned for his own honour, and though the things considered honourable may have shifted or been enlarged, loyalty to word and to allegiance, and un-flinching courage remain. These are tested in adventures no nearer to ordinary life than Grendel or the dragon; but Gawain's conduct is made more worthy, and more worth considering, again because he is a subordinate. He is involved in peril and the certain prospect of death simply by loyalty, and the desire to secure the safety and dignity of his lord, King Arthur. And upon him depends in his quest the honour of his lord and of his *heorðwerod,* the Round Table. It is no accident that in this poem, as in *Maldon* and in *Beowulf,* we have criticism of the lord, of the owner of the allegiance. The words are striking, though less so than the small part they have played in criticism of the poem (as also in *Maldon*). Yet thus spoke the court of the great King Arthur, when Sir Gawain rode away:

[1] It is probably the first work to apply the word "letters" to this metre, which has in fact never regarded them.

> *Before God 'tis a shame*
> *that thou, lord, must be lost, who art in life so noble!*
> *To meet his match among men, Marry, 'tis not easy!*
> *To behave with more heed would have behoved one of sense,*
> *and that dear lord duly a duke to have made,*
> *illustrious leader of liegemen in this land as befits him;*
> *and that better would have been than to be butchered to death,*
> *beheaded by an elvish man for an arrogant vaunt.*
> *Who ever heard tell of a king such courses taking,*
> *as knights quibbling at court at their Christmas games!*

*Beowulf* is a rich poem; there are of course many other sides to the description of the manner of the hero's death; and the consideration (sketched above) of the changing values of chivalry in youth and in age and responsibility is only an ingredient. Yet it is plainly there; and though the author's main imagination was moving in wider ways, criticism of the lord and owner of the allegiance is touched on.

Thus the lord may indeed receive credit from the deeds of his knights, but he must not use their loyalty or imperil them simply for that purpose. It was not Hygelac that sent Beowulf to Denmark through any boast or rash vow. His words to Beowulf on his return are no doubt an alteration of the older story (which peeps rather through in the egging of the *snotere ceorlas,* 202–4); but they are the more significant for that. We hear, 1992–7, that Hygelac had tried to restrain Beowulf from a rash adventure. Very properly. But at the end the situation is reversed. We learn, 3076–83, that Wiglaf and the Geatas regarded any attack on the dragon as rash, and had tried to restrain the king from the perilous enterprise, with words very like those used by Hygelac long before. But the king wished for glory, or for a glorious death, and courted disaster. There could be no more pungent criticism in a few words of "chivalry" in one of responsibility than Wiglaf's exclamation: *oft sceall eorl monig anes willan wraec adreogan,* "by one man's will many must woe endure". These words the poet of Maldon might have inscribed at the head of his work.

# TREE AND LEAF

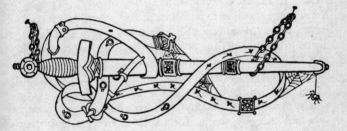

## ON FAIRY STORIES
*page 3*

## LEAF BY NIGGLE
*page 87*

# INTRODUCTORY NOTE

THESE two things, *On Fairy-stories* and *Leaf by Niggle,* are here reprinted and issued together. They are no longer easy to obtain, but they may still be found interesting, especially by those to whom *The Lord of the Rings* has given pleasure. Though one is an "essay" and the other a "story", they are related: by the symbols of Tree and Leaf, and by both touching in different ways on what is called in the essay "sub-creation." Also they were written in the same period (1938-39), when *The Lord of the Rings* was beginning to unroll itself and to unfold prospects of labour and exploration in yet unknown country as daunting to me as to the hobbits. At about that time we had reached Bree, and I had then no more notion than they had of what had become of Gandalf or who Strider was; and I had begun to despair of surviving to find out.

The essay was originally composed as an Andrew Lang Lecture and was in a shorter form delivered in the University of St. Andrews in 1938.[1] It was eventually published, with a little enlargement, as one of the items in *Essays presented to Charles Williams,* Oxford University Press, 1947, now out of print. It is here reproduced with only a few minor alterations.

The story was not published until 1947 (*Dublin Review*). It has not been changed since it reached manuscript form, very swiftly, one day when I awoke with it already in mind. One of its sources was a great-limbed poplar tree that I could see even lying in bed. It was suddenly lopped and mutilated by its owner, I do not know why. It is cut down now, a less barbarous punishment for any crimes it may have been accused of, such as being large and alive. I do not think it had any friends, or any mourners, except myself and a pair of owls.

J. R. R. TOLKIEN

[1] Not 1940 as incorrectly stated in 1947.

# ON FAIRY-STORIES

I PROPOSE to speak about fairy-stories, though I am aware that this is a rash adventure. Faërie is a perilous land, and in it are pitfalls for the unwary and dungeons for the overbold. And overbold I may be accounted, for though I have been a lover of fairy-stories since I learned to read, and have at times thought about them, I have not studied them professionally. I have been hardly more than a wandering explorer (or trespasser) in the land, full of wonder but not of information.

The realm of fairy-story is wide and deep and high and filled with many things: all manner of beasts and birds are found there; shoreless seas and stars uncounted; beauty that is an enchantment, and an ever-present peril; both joy and sorrow as sharp as swords. In that realm a man may, perhaps, count himself fortunate to have wandered, but its very richness and strangeness tie the tongue of a traveller who would report them. And while he is there it is dangerous for him to ask too many questions, lest the gates should be shut and the keys be lost.

There are, however, some questions that one who is to speak about fairy-stories must expect to answer, or attempt to answer, whatever the folk of Faërie may think of his impertinence. For instance: What are fairy-stories? What is their origin? What is the use of them? I will try to give answers to these questions, or such hints of answers to them as I have gleaned — primarily from the stories themselves, the few of all their multitude that I know.

### FAIRY-STORY

What is a fairy-story? In this case you will turn to the *Oxford English Dictionary* in vain. It contains no reference to the combination *fairy-story*, and is unhelpful on the subject of *fairies* generally. In the Supplement, *fairy-tale* is recorded since the year 1750, and its leading sense is said to be (*a*) a tale about fairies, or generally a fairy legend; with developed senses, (*b*) an unreal or incredible story, and (*c*) a falsehood.

The last two senses would obviously make my topic hopelessly vast. But the first sense is too narrow. Not too narrow for an essay; it is wide enough for many books, but too narrow to cover actual usage. Especially so, if we accept the lexicographer's definition of *fairies:* "supernatural beings of diminutive size, in popular belief supposed to possess magical powers and to have great influence for good or evil over the affairs of man."

*Supernatural* is a dangerous and difficult word in any of its senses, looser or stricter. But to fairies it can hardly be applied, unless *super* is taken merely as a su·

perlative prefix. For it is man who is, in contrast to
fairies, supernatural (and often of diminutive stature);
whereas they are natural, far more natural than he.
Such is their doom. The road to fairyland is not the
road to Heaven; nor even to Hell, I believe, though
some have held that it may lead thither indirectly by
the Devil's tithe.

> O see ye not yon narrow road
>   So thick beset wi' thorns and briers?
> That is the path of Righteousness,
>   Though after it but few inquires.
>
> And see ye not yon braid, braid road
>   That lies across the lily leven?
> That is the path of Wickedness,
>   Though some call it the Road to Heaven.
>
> And see ye not yon bonny road
>   That winds about yon fernie brae?
> That is the road to fair Elfland,
>   Where thou and I this night maun gae.

As for *diminutive size:* I do not deny that the notion
is a leading one in modern use. I have often thought
that it would be interesting to try to find out how that
has come to be so; but my knowledge is not sufficient for
a certain answer. Of old there were indeed some inhabitants of Faërie that were small (though hardly diminutive), but smallness was not characteristic of that
people as a whole. The diminutive being, elf or fairy, is
(I guess) in England largely a sophisticated product of

literary fancy.[1] It is perhaps not unnatural that in England, the land where the love of the delicate and fine has often reappeared in art, fancy should in this matter turn towards the dainty and diminutive, as in France it went to court and put on powder and diamonds. Yet I suspect that this flower-and-butterfly minuteness was also a product of "rationalization," which transformed the glamour of Elfland into mere finesse, and invisibility into a fragility that could hide in a cowslip or shrink behind a blade of grass. It seems to become fashionable soon after the great voyages had begun to make the world seem too narrow to hold both men and elves; when the magic land of Hy Breasail in the West had become the mere Brazils, the land of red-dye-wood.[2] In any case it was largely a literary business in which William Shakespeare and Michael Drayton played a part.[3] Drayton's *Nymphidia* is one ancestor of that long line of flower-fairies and fluttering sprites with antennae that I so disliked as a child, and which my children in their turn detested. Andrew Lang had similar feelings. In the preface to the *Lilac Fairy Book* he refers to the tales of tiresome contemporary authors: "they always

[1] I am speaking of developments before the growth of interest in the folk-lore of other countries. The English words, such as *elf*, have long been influenced by French (from which *fay* and *faërie*, *fairy* are derived); but in later times, through their use in translation, both *fairy* and *elf* have acquired much of the atmosphere of German, Scandinavian, and Celtic tales, and many characteristics of the *huldu-fólk*, the *daoine-sithe*, and the *tylwyth teg*.

[2] For the probability that the Irish *Hy Breasail* played a part in the naming of Brazil see Nansen, *In Northern Mists*, ii, 223-30.

[3] Their influence was not confined to England. German *Elf, Elfe* appears to be derived from *A Midsummer-night's Dream*, in Wieland's translation (1764).

begin with a little boy or girl who goes out and meets the fairies of polyanthuses and gardenias and apple-blossom. . . . These fairies try to be funny and fail; or they try to preach and succeed."

But the business began, as I have said, long before the nineteenth century, and long ago achieved tiresomeness, certainly the tiresomeness of trying to be funny and failing. Drayton's *Nymphidia* is, considered as a fairy-story (a story about fairies), one of the worst ever written. The palace of Oberon has walls of spider's legs,

> *And windows of the eyes of cats,*
> *And for the roof, instead of slats,*
> *Is covered with the wings of bats.*

The knight Pigwiggen rides on a frisky earwig, and sends his love, Queen Mab, a bracelet of emmets' eyes, making an assignation in a cowslip-flower. But the tale that is told amid all this prettiness is a dull story of intrigue and sly go-betweens; the gallant knight and angry husband fall into the mire, and their wrath is stilled by a draught of the waters of Lethe. It would have been better if Lethe had swallowed the whole affair. Oberon, Mab, and Pigwiggen may be diminutive elves or fairies, as Arthur, Guinevere, and Lancelot are not; but the good and evil story of Arthur's court is a "fairy-story" rather than this tale of Oberon.

*Fairy*, as a noun more or less equivalent to *elf*, is a relatively modern word, hardly used until the Tudor period. The first quotation in the *Oxford Dictionary* (the only one before A.D. 1450) is significant. It is taken

from the poet Gower: *as he were a faierie.* But this
Gower did not say. He wrote *as he were of faierie,* "as
if he were come from Faërie." Gower was describing
a young gallant who seeks to bewitch the hearts of the
maidens in church.

> *His croket kembd and thereon set*
> *A Nouche with a chapelet,*
> *Or elles one of grene leves*
> *Which late com out of the greves,*
> *Al for he sholde seme freissh;*
> *And thus he loketh on the fleissh,*
> *Riht as an hauk which hath a sihte*
> *Upon the foul ther he schal lihte,*
> *And as he were of faierie*
> *He scheweth him tofore here yhe.*[4]

This is a young man of mortal blood and bone; but he
gives a much better picture of the inhabitants of Elfland than the definition of a "fairy" under which he is,
by a double error, placed. For the trouble with the real
folk of Faërie is that they do not always look like what
they are; and they put on the pride and beauty that we
would fain wear ourselves. At least part of the magic
that they wield for the good or evil of man is power to
play on the desires of his body and his heart. The
Queen of Elfland, who carried off Thomas the Rhymer
upon her milk-white steed swifter than the wind, came
riding by the Eildon Tree as a lady, if one of enchanting
beauty. So that Spenser was in the true tradition when
he called the knights of his Faërie by the name of Elfe.

[4] *Confessio Amantis,* v. 7065 ff.

It belonged to such knights as Sir Guyon rather than to Pigwiggen armed with a hornet's sting.

Now, though I have only touched (wholly inadequately) on *elves* and *fairies,* I must turn back; for I have digressed from my proper theme: fairy-stories. I said the sense "stories about fairies" was too narrow.[5] It is too narrow, even if we reject the diminutive size, for fairy-stories are not in normal English usage stories *about* fairies or elves, but stories about Fairy, that is *Faërie,* the realm or state in which fairies have their being. *Faërie* contains many things besides elves and fays, and besides dwarfs, witches, trolls, giants, or dragons: it holds the seas, the sun, the moon, the sky; and the earth, and all things that are in it: tree and bird, water and stone, wine and bread, and ourselves, mortal men, when we are enchanted.

Stories that are actually concerned primarily with "fairies," that is with creatures that might also in modern English be called "elves," are relatively rare, and as a rule not very interesting. Most good "fairy-stories" are about the *aventures* of men in the Perilous Realm or upon its shadowy marches. Naturally so; for if elves are true, and really exist independently of our tales about them, then this also is certainly true: elves are not primarily concerned with us, nor we with them. Our fates are sundered, and our paths seldom meet. Even upon

[5] Except in special cases such as collections of Welsh or Gaelic tales. In these the stories about the "Fair Family" or the Shee-folk are sometimes distinguished as "fairy-tales" from "folk-tales" concerning other marvels. In this use "fairy-tales" or "fairy-lore" are usually short accounts of the appearances of "fairies" or their intrusions upon the affairs of men. But this distinction is a product of translation.

the borders of Faërie we encounter them only at some chance crossing of the ways.[6]

The definition of a fairy-story — what it is, or what it should be — does not, then, depend on any definition or historical account of elf or fairy, but upon the nature of *Faërie:* the Perilous Realm itself, and the air that blows in that country. I will not attempt to define that, nor to describe it directly. It cannot be done. Faërie cannot be caught in a net of words; for it is one of its qualities to be indescribable, though not imperceptible. It has many ingredients, but analysis will not necessarily discover the secret of the whole. Yet I hope that what I have later to say about the other questions will give some glimpses of my own imperfect vision of it. For the moment I will say only this: a "fairy-story" is one which touches on or uses Faërie, whatever its own main purpose may be: satire, adventure, morality, fantasy. Faërie itself may perhaps most nearly be translated by Magic[7] — but it is magic of a peculiar mood and power, at the furthest pole from the vulgar devices of the laborious, scientific, magician. There is one proviso: if there is any satire present in the tale, one thing must not be made fun of, the magic itself. That must in that story be taken seriously, neither laughed at nor explained away. Of this seriousness the medieval *Sir Gawain and the Green Knight* is an admirable example.

But even if we apply only these vague and ill-defined limits, it becomes plain that many, even the learned in

[6] This is true also, even if they are only creations of Man's mind, "true" only as reflecting in a particular way one of Man's visions of Truth.

[7] See further below, p. 52.

such matters, have used the term "fairy-tale" very carelessly. A glance at those books of recent times that claim to be collections of "fairy-stories" is enough to show that tales about fairies, about the fair family in any of its houses, or even about dwarfs and goblins, are only a small part of their content. That, as we have seen, was to be expected. But these books also contain many tales that do not use, do not even touch upon, Faërie at all; that have in fact no business to be included.

I will give one or two examples of the expurgations I would perform. This will assist the negative side of definition. It will also be found to lead on to the second question: what are the origins of fairy-stories?

The number of collections of fairy-stories is now very great. In English none probably rival either the popularity, or the inclusiveness, or the general merits of the twelve books of twelve colours which we owe to Andrew Lang and to his wife. The first of these appeared more than seventy years ago (1889), and is still in print. Most of its contents pass the test, more or less clearly. I will not analyse them, though an analysis might be interesting, but I note in passing that of the stories in this *Blue Fairy Book* none are primarily about "fairies," few refer to them. Most of the tales are taken from French sources: a just choice in some ways at that time, as perhaps it would be still (though not to my taste, now or in childhood). At any rate, so powerful has been the influence of Charles Perrault, since his *Contes de ma Mère l'Oye* were first Englished in the eighteenth century, and of such other excerpts from the vast storehouse of the *Cabinet des Fées* as have become well known, that still, I suppose, if you asked a man to name at random a typical "fairy-story," he would be most likely to name one of these French things: such as *Puss-in-Boots, Cinderella,* or *Little Red Riding Hood.* With some people *Grimm's Fairy Tales* might come first to mind.

But what is to be said of the appearance in the *Blue Fairy Book* of *A Voyage to Lilliput?* I will say this: it is *not* a fairy-story, neither as its author made it, nor as it here appears "condensed" by Miss May Kendall. It has no business in this place. I fear that it was included merely because Lilliputians are small, even diminutive — the only way in which they are at all remarkable. But smallness is in Faërie, as in our world, only an accident. Pygmies are no nearer to fairies than are Patagonians. I do not rule this story out because of its satirical intent: there is satire, sustained or intermittent, in undoubted fairy-stories, and satire may often have been intended in traditional tales where we do not now perceive it. I rule it out, because the vehicle of the satire, brilliant invention though it may be, belongs to the class of travellers' tales. Such tales report many marvels, but they are marvels to be seen in this mortal world in some region of our own time and space; distance alone conceals them. The tales of Gulliver have no more right of entry than the yarns of Baron Munchausen; or than, say, *The First Men in the Moon* or *The Time-Machine.* Indeed, for the Eloi and the Morlocks there would be a better claim than for the Lilliputians. Lilliputians are merely men peered down at, sardonically, from just above the house-tops. Eloi and Morlocks live far away in an abyss of time so deep as to work an enchantment upon them; and if they are descended from ourselves, it may be remembered that an ancient English thinker once derived the *ylfe*, the very elves, through Cain from Adam.[8] This enchantment of distance, especially of distant time, is weakened only by the preposterous and incredible Time Machine itself. But we see in this example one of the main reasons why the borders of fairy-story are inevitably dubious. The magic of Faërie is not an end in itself, its virtue is in its operations: among these are the satisfaction of certain primordial human desires. One of these desires is to survey the depths of space and time. Another is (as will be seen) to hold communion with other living things. A story may thus deal with the satisfaction of these desires, with or without the operation of either machine or magic, and in proportion as it succeeds it will approach the quality and have the flavour of fairy-story.

Next, after travellers' tales, I would also exclude, or rule out of order, any story that uses the machinery of Dream, the dreaming of actual human sleep, to explain the apparent occurrence of its marvels. At the least, even if the reported dream was in other respects in itself a fairy-story, I would condemn the whole as gravely defective: like a good picture in a disfiguring frame. It is true that Dream is not unconnected with Faërie. In dreams strange powers of the mind may be unlocked. In some of them a man may for a space wield the power of Faërie, that power which, even as it

8 *Beowulf*, 111-12.

conceives the story, causes it to take living form and
colour before the eyes. A real dream may indeed sometimes be a fairy-story of almost elvish ease and skill —
while it is being dreamed. But if a waking writer tells
you that his tale is only a thing imagined in his sleep, he
cheats deliberately the primal desire at the heart of
Faërie: the realization, independent of the conceiving
mind, of imagined wonder. It is often reported of fairies (truly or lyingly, I do not know) that they are work-
ers of illusion, that they are cheaters of men by "fantasy"; but that is quite another matter. That is their
affair. Such trickeries happen, at any rate, inside tales
in which the fairies are not themselves illusions; behind
the fantasy real wills and powers exist, independent of
the minds and purposes of men.

It is at any rate essential to a genuine fairy-story, as
distinct from the employment of this form for lesser or
debased purposes, that it should be presented as "true."
The meaning of "true" in this connexion I will consider
in a moment. But since the fairy-story deals with "marvels," it cannot tolerate any frame or machinery sug-
gesting that the whole story in which they occur is a fig-
ment or illusion. The tale itself may, of course, be so
good that one can ignore the frame. Or it may be successful and amusing as a dream-story. So are Lewis
Carroll's *Alice* stories, with their dream-frame and
dream-transitions. For this (and other reasons) they
are not fairy-stories.[9]

There is another type of marvellous tale that I would
exclude from the title "fairy-story," again certainly not

[9] See Note A at the end (p. 75).

because I do not like it: namely pure "Beast-fable." I will choose an example from Lang's Fairy Books: *The Monkey's Heart*, a Swahili tale which is given in the *Lilac Fairy Book*. In this story a wicked shark tricked a monkey into riding on his back, and carried him half-way to his own land, before he revealed the fact that the sultan of that country was sick and needed a monkey's heart to cure his disease. But the monkey outwitted the shark, and induced him to return by convincing him that the heart had been left behind at home, hanging in a bag on a tree.

The beast-fable has, of course, a connexion with fairy-stories. Beasts and birds and other creatures often talk like men in real fairy-stories. In some part (often small) this marvel derives from one of the primal "desires" that lie near the heart of Faërie: the desire of men to hold communion with other living things. But the speech of beasts in a beast-fable, as developed into a separate branch, has little reference to that desire, and often wholly forgets it. The magical understanding by men of the proper languages of birds and beasts and trees, that is much nearer to the true purposes of Faërie. But in stories in which no human being is concerned; or in which the animals are the heroes and heroines, and men and women, if they appear, are mere adjuncts; and above all those in which the animal form is only a mask upon a human face, a device of the satirist or the preacher, in these we have beast-fable and not fairy-story: whether it be *Reynard the Fox*, or *The Nun's Priest's Tale*, or *Brer Rabbit*, or merely *The Three Little Pigs*. The stories of Beatrix Potter lie near the borders

of Faërie, but outside it, I think, for the most part.[10]
Their nearness is due largely to their strong moral element: by which I mean their inherent morality, not any
allegorical *significatio*. But *Peter Rabbit*, though it contains a prohibition, and though there are prohibitions in
fairyland (as, probably, there are throughout the uni-
verse on every plane and in every dimension), remains
a beast-fable.

Now *The Monkey's Heart* is also plainly only a beast-
fable. I suspect that its inclusion in a "Fairy Book" is
due not primarily to its entertaining quality, but precisely to the monkey's heart supposed to have been left
behind in a bag. That was significant to Lang, the student of folk-lore, even though this curious idea is here
used only as a joke; for, in this tale, the monkey's heart
was in fact quite normal and in his breast. None the
less this detail is plainly only a secondary use of an ancient and very widespread folk-lore notion, which does
occur in fairy-stories; [11] the notion that the life or
strength of a man or creature may reside in some other
place or thing; or in some part of the body (especially
the heart) that can be detached and hidden in a bag, or
under a stone, or in an egg. At one end of recorded folk-
lore history this idea was used by George MacDonald
in his fairy-story *The Giant's Heart*, which derives this
central motive (as well as many other details) from

[10] *The Tailor of Gloucester* perhaps comes nearest. *Mrs. Tiggy-
winkle* would be as near, but for the hinted dream-explanation. I
would also include *The Wind in the Willows* in Beast-fable.

[11] Such as, for instance: *The Giant that had no Heart* in Dasent's
*Popular Tales from the Norse;* or *The Sea-Maiden* in Campbell's *Popular Tales of the West Highlands* (no. iv, cf. also no. i); or more re-
motely *Die Kristallkugel* in Grimm.

well-known traditional tales. At the other end, indeed in what is probably one of the oldest stories in writing, it occurs in *The Tale of the Two Brothers* on the Egyptian D'Orsigny papyrus. There the younger brother says to the elder:

> I shall enchant my heart, and I shall place it upon the top of the flower of the cedar. Now the cedar will be cut down and my heart will fall to the ground, and thou shalt come to seek for it, even though thou pass seven years in seeking it; but when thou has found it, put it into a vase of cold water, and in very truth I shall live.[12]

But that point of interest and such comparisons as these bring us to the brink of the second question: What are the origins of "fairy-stories"? That must, of course, mean: the origin or origins of the fairy elements. To ask what is the origin of stories (however qualified) is to ask what is the origin of language and of the mind.

### ORIGINS

Actually the question: What is the origin of the fairy element? lands us ultimately in the same fundamental inquiry; but there are many elements in fairy-stories (such as this detachable heart, or swan-robes, magic rings, arbitrary prohibitions, wicked stepmothers, and even fairies themselves) that can be studied without

[12] Budge, *Egyptian Reading Book*, p. xxi.

tackling this main question. Such studies are, however, scientific (at least in intent); they are the pursuit of folklorists or anthropologists: that is of people using the stories not as they were meant to be used, but as a quarry from which to dig evidence, or information, about matters in which they are interested. A perfectly legitimate procedure in itself — but ignorance or forgetfulness of the nature of a story (as a thing told in its entirety) has often led such inquirers into strange judgements. To investigators of this sort recurring similarities (such as this matter of the heart) seem specially important. So much so that students of folk-lore are apt to get off their own proper track, or to express themselves in a misleading "shorthand": misleading in particular, if it gets out of their monographs into books about literature. They are inclined to say that any two stories that are built round the same folk-lore motive, or are made up of a generally similar combination of such motives, are "the same stories." We read that *Beowulf* "is only a version of *Dat Erdmänneken*"; that "*The Black Bull of Norroway* is *Beauty and the Beast*," or "is the same story as *Eros and Psyche*"; that the Norse *Mastermaid* (or the Gaelic *Battle of the Birds*[13] and its many congeners and variants) is "the same story as the Greek tale of Jason and Medea."

Statements of that kind may express (in undue abbreviation) some element of truth; but they are not true in a fairy-story sense, they are not true in art or literature. It is precisely the colouring, the atmosphere, the unclassifiable individual details of a story, and above all

[13] See Campbell, op. cit., vol. i.

the general purport that informs with life the undissected bones of the plot, that really count. Shakespeare's *King Lear* is not the same as Layamon's story in his *Brut*. Or to take the extreme case of *Red Riding Hood*: it is of merely secondary interest that the re-told versions of this story, in which the little girl is saved by wood-cutters, is directly derived from Perrault's story in which she was eaten by the wolf. The really important thing is that the later version has a happy ending (more or less, and if we do not mourn the grandmother overmuch), and that Perrault's version had not. And that is a very profound difference, to which I shall return.

Of course, I do not deny, for I feel strongly, the fascination of the desire to unravel the intricately knotted and ramified history of the branches on the Tree of Tales. It is closely connected with the philologists' study of the tangled skein of Language, of which I know some small pieces. But even with regard to language it seems to me that the essential quality and aptitudes of a given language in a living monument is both more important to seize and far more difficult to make explicit than its linear history. So with regard to fairy stories, I feel that it is more interesting, and also in its way more difficult, to consider what they are, what they have become for us, and what values the long alchemic processes of time have produced in them. In Dasent's words I would say: "We must be satisfied with the soup that is set before us, and not desire to see the bones of the ox out of which it has been boiled." [14] Though,

14 *Popular Tales from the Norse*, p. xviii.

oddly enough, Dasent by "the soup" meant a mishmash of bogus pre-history founded on the early surmises of Comparative Philology; and by "desire to see the bones" he meant a demand to see the workings and the proofs that led to these theories. By "the soup" I mean the story as it is served up by its author or teller, and by "the bones" its sources or material — even when (by rare luck) those can be with certainty discovered. But I do not, of course, forbid criticism of the soup as soup.

I shall therefore pass lightly over the question of origins. I am too unlearned to deal with it in any other way; but it is the least important of the three questions for my purpose, and a few remarks will suffice. It is plain enough that fairy-stories (in wider or in narrower sense) are very ancient indeed. Related things appear in very early records; and they are found universally, wherever there is language. We are therefore obviously confronted with a variant of the problem that the archaeologist encounters, or the comparative philologist: with the debate between *independent evolution* (or rather *invention*) of the similar; *inheritance* from a common ancestry; and *diffusion* at various times from one or more centres. Most debates depend on an attempt (by one or both sides) at over-simplification; and I do not suppose that this debate is an exception. The history of fairy-stories is probably more complex than the physical history of the human race, and as complex as the history of human language. All three things: independent invention, inheritance, and diffusion, have evidently played their part in producing the intricate web of Story. It is now beyond all skill but that of the elves to unravel it.[15] Of these three *invention* is the most important and fundamental, and so (not surprisingly) also the most mysterious. To an inventor, that is to a storymaker, the other two must in the end lead back. *Diffusion* (borrowing in space) whether of an artefact or a story, only refers the problem of origin elsewhere. At the centre of the supposed diffusion there is a place where once an inventor lived. Similarly with *inheritance* (borrowing in time): in this way we arrive at last only at an ancestral inventor. While if we believe that sometimes there occurred the independent striking out of similar ideas and themes or devices, we simply multiply the ancestral inventor but do not in that way the more clearly understand his gift.

Philology has been dethroned from the high place it once had in this court of inquiry. Max Müller's view of mythology as a "disease of language" can be abandoned without regret. Mythology is not a disease at all, though it may like all human things become diseased. You might as well say that thinking is a disease of the mind. It would be more near the truth to say that languages, especially modern European languages, are a disease of mythology. But Language cannot, all the same, be dismissed. The incarnate mind, the tongue,

---

[15] Except in particularly fortunate cases; or in a few occasional details. It is indeed easier to unravel a single *thread* — an incident, a name, a motive — than to trace the history of any *picture* defined by many threads. For with the picture in the tapestry a new element has come in: the picture is greater than, and not explained by, the sum of the component threads. Therein lies the inherent weakness of the analytic (or "scientific") method: it finds out much about things that occur in stories, but little or nothing about their effect in any given story.

and the tale are in our world coeval. The human mind, endowed with the powers of generalization and abstraction, sees not only *green-grass*, discriminating it from other things (and finding it fair to look upon), but sees that it is *green* as well as being *grass*. But how powerful, how stimulating to the very faculty that produced it, was the invention of the adjective: no spell or incantation in Faërie is more potent. And that is not surprising: such incantations might indeed be said to be only another view of adjectives, a part of speech in a mythical grammar. The mind that thought of *light, heavy, grey, yellow, still, swift*, also conceived of magic that would make heavy things light and able to fly, turn grey lead into yellow gold, and the still rock into a swift water. If it could do the one, it could do the other; it inevitably did both. When we can take green from grass, blue from heaven, and red from blood, we have already an enchanter's power — upon one plane; and the desire to wield that power in the world external to our minds awakes. It does not follow that we shall use that power well upon any plane. We may put a deadly green upon a man's face and produce a horror; we may make the rare and terrible blue moon to shine; or we may cause woods to spring with silver leaves and rams to wear fleeces of gold, and put hot fire into the belly of the cold worm. But in such "fantasy," as it is called, new form is made; Faërie begins; Man becomes a sub-creator.

An essential power of Faërie is thus the power of making immediately effective by the will the visions of "fantasy." Not all are beautiful or even wholesome, not at any rate the fantasies of fallen Man. And he has stained the elves who have this power (in verity or fable) with his own stain. This aspect of "mythology" — sub-creation, rather than either representation or symbolic interpretation of the beauties and terrors of the world — is, I think, too little considered. Is that because it is seen rather in Faërie than upon Olympus? Because it is thought to belong to the "lower mythology" rather than to the "higher"? There has been much debate concerning the relations of these things, of *folk-tale* and *myth;* but, even if there had been no debate, the question would require some notice in any consideration of origins, however brief.

At one time it was a dominant view that all such matter was derived from "nature-myths." The Olympians were *personifications* of the sun, of dawn, of night, and so on, and all the stories told about them were originally *myths* (*allegories* would have been a better word) of the greater elemental changes and processes of nature. Epic, heroic legend, saga, then localized these stories in real places and humanized them by attributing them to ancestral heroes, mightier than men and yet already men. And finally these legends, dwindling down, became folk-tales, *Märchen,* fairy-stories — nursery-tales.

That would seem to be the truth almost upside down. The nearer the so-called "nature myth," or allegory, of the large processes of nature is to its supposed archetype, the less interesting it is, and indeed the less is it of a myth capable of throwing any illumination whatever on the world. Let us assume for the moment, as this theory assumes, that nothing actually exists corresponding to the "gods" of mythology: no personalities, only astronomical or meteorological objects. Then these natural objects can only be arrayed with a personal significance and glory by a gift, the gift of a person, of a man. Personality can only be derived from a person. The gods may derive their colour and beauty from the high splendours of nature, but it was Man who obtained these for them, abstracted them from sun and moon and cloud; their personality they get direct from him; the shadow or flicker of divinity that is upon them they receive through him from the invisible world, the Supernatural. There is no fundamental distinction between the higher and lower mythologies. Their peoples live, if they live at all, by the same life, just as in the mortal world do kings and peasants.

Let us take what looks like a clear case of Olympian nature-myth: the Norse god Thórr. His name is Thunder, of which Thórr is the Norse form; and it is not difficult to interpret his hammer, Miöllnir, as lightning. Yet Thórr has (as far as our late records go) a very marked character, or personality, which cannot be found in thunder or in lightning, even though some details can, as it were, be related to these natural phenomena: for instance, his red beard, his loud voice and violent temper, his blundering and smashing strength. None the less it is asking a question without much meaning, if we inquire: Which came first, nature-allegories about personalized thunder in the mountains, splitting rocks and trees; or stories about an irascible, not very clever, red-beard farmer, of a strength beyond common measure, a person (in all but mere stature) very like the Northern farmers, the *bœndr* by whom Thórr was chiefly beloved? To a picture of such a man Thórr may be held to have "dwindled," or from it the god may be held to have been enlarged. But I doubt whether either view is right — not by itself, not if you insist that one of these things must precede the other. It is more reasonable to suppose that the farmer popped up in the very moment when Thunder got a voice and face; that there was a distant growl of thunder in the hills every time a storyteller heard a farmer in a rage.

Thórr must, of course, be reckoned a member of the higher aristocracy of mythology: one of the rulers of the world. Yet the tale that is told of him in *Thrymskvitha* (in the Elder Edda) is certainly just a fairy-story. It is old, as far as Norse poems go, but that is not far back (say A.D. 900 or a little earlier, in this case). But there is no real reason for supposing that this tale is "unprimitive," at any rate in quality: that is, because it is of folktale kind and not very dignified. If we could go backwards in time, the fairy-story might be found to change in details, or to give way to other tales. But there would always be a "fairy-tale" as long as there was any Thórr. When the fairy-tale ceased, there would be just thunder, which no human ear had yet heard.

Something really "higher" is occasionally glimpsed in mythology: Divinity, the right to power (as distinct from its possession), the due of worship; in fact "religion." Andrew Lang said, and is by some still commended for saying,[16] that mythology and religion (in

16 For example, by Christopher Dawson in *Progress and Religion*.

the strict sense of that word) are two distinct things that have become inextricably entangled, though mythology is in itself almost devoid of religious significance.[17]

Yet these things have in fact become entangled — or maybe they were sundered long ago and have since groped slowly, through a labyrinth of error, through confusion, back towards re-fusion. Even fairy-stories as a whole have three faces: the Mystical towards the Supernatural; the Magical towards Nature; and the Mirror of scorn and pity towards Man. The essential face of Faërie is the middle one, the Magical. But the degree in which the others appear (if at all) is variable, and may be decided by the individual story-teller. The Magical, the fairy-story, may be used as a *Mirour de l'Omme;* and it may (but not so easily) be made a vehicle of Mystery. This at least is what George MacDonald attempted, achieving stories of power and beauty when he succeeded, as in *The Golden Key* (which he called a fairy-tale); and even when he partly failed, as in *Lilith* (which he called a romance).

For a moment let us return to the "Soup" that I mentioned above. Speaking of the history of stories and especially of fairy-stories we may say that the Pot of Soup, the Cauldron of Story, has always been boiling,

[17] This is borne out by the more careful and sympathetic study of "primitive" peoples: that is, peoples still living in an inherited paganism, who are not, as we say, civilized. The hasty survey finds only their wilder tales; a closer examination finds their cosmological myths; only patience and inner knowledge discovers their philosophy and religion: the truly worshipful, of which the "gods" are not necessarily an embodiment at all, or only in a variable measure (often decided by the individual).

and to it have continually been added new bits, dainty and undainty. For this reason, to take a casual example, the fact that a story resembling the one known as *The Goosegirl* (*Die Gänsemagd* in Grimm) is told in the thirteenth century of Bertha Broadfoot, mother of Charlemagne, really proves nothing either way: neither that the story was (in the thirteenth century) descending from Olympus or Asgard by way of an already legendary king of old, on its way to become a *Hausmärchen;* nor that it was on its way up. The story is found to be widespread, unattached to the mother of Charlemagne or to any historical character. From this fact by itself we certainly cannot deduce that it is not true of Charlemagne's mother, though that is the kind of deduction that is most frequently made from that kind of evidence. The opinion that the story is not true of Bertha Broadfoot must be founded on something else: on features in the story which the critic's philosophy does not allow to be possible in "real life," so that he would actually disbelieve the tale, even if it were found nowhere else; or on the existence of good historical evidence that Bertha's actual life was quite different, so that he would disbelieve the tale, even if his philosophy allowed that it was perfectly possible in "real life." No one, I fancy, would discredit a story that the Archbishop of Canterbury slipped on a banana skin merely because he found that a similar comic mishap had been reported of many people, and especially of elderly gentlemen of dignity. He might disbelieve the story, if he discovered that in it an angel (or even a fairy) had warned the Archbishop that he would slip if he wore

gaiters on a Friday. He might also disbelieve the story,
if it was stated to have occurred in the period between,
say, 1940 and 1945. So much for that. It is an obvious
point, and it has been made before; but I venture to
make it again (although it is a little beside my present
purpose), for it is constantly neglected by those who
concern themselves with the origins of tales.

But what of the banana skin? Our business with it
really only begins when it has been rejected by historians. It is more useful when it has been thrown away.
The historian would be likely to say that the banana-
skin story "became attached to the Archbishop," as he
does say on fair evidence that "the Goosegirl *Märchen*
became attached to Bertha." That way of putting it is
harmless enough, in what is commonly known as "history." But is it really a good description of what is going on and has gone on in the history of story-making?
I do not think so. I think it would be nearer the truth to
say that the Archbishop became attached to the banana
skin, or that Bertha was turned into the Goosegirl. Better still: I would say that Charlemagne's mother and
the Archbishop were put into the Pot, in fact got into
the Soup. They were just new bits added to the stock.
A considerable honour, for in that soup were many
things older, more potent, more beautiful, comic, or terrible than they were in themselves (considered simply
as figures of history).

It seems fairly plain that Arthur, once historical (but
perhaps as such not of great importance), was also put
into the Pot. There he was boiled for a long time, together with many other older figures and devices, of

mythology and Faerie, and even some other stray bones
of history (such as Alfred's defence against the Danes),
until he emerged as a King of Faërie. The situation is
similar in the great Northern "Arthurian" court of the
Shield-Kings of Denmark, the *Scyldingas* of ancient
English tradition. King Hrothgar and his family have
many manifest marks of true history, far more than Arthur; yet even in the older (English) accounts of them
they are associated with many figures and events of
fairy-story: they have been in the Pot. But I refer now
to the remnants of the oldest recorded English tales of
Faërie (or its borders), in spite of the fact that they are
little known in England, not to discuss the turning of
the bear-boy into the knight Beowulf, or to explain the
intrusion of the ogre Grendel into the royal hall of
Hrothgar. I wish to point to something else that these
traditions contain: a singularly suggestive example of
the relation of the "fairy-tale element" to gods and kings
and nameless men, illustrating (I believe) the view that
this element does not rise or fall, but is there, in the
Cauldron of Story, waiting for the great figures of Myth
and History, and for the yet nameless He or She, waiting
for the moment when they are cast into the simmering
stew, one by one or all together, without consideration
of rank or precedence.

The great enemy of King Hròthgar was Froda, King
of the Heathobards. Yet of Hrothgar's daughter Freawaru we hear echoes of a strange tale — not a usual one
in Northern heroic legend: the son of the enemy of her
house, Ingeld son of Froda, fell in love with her and
wedded her, disastrously. But that is extremely inter-

esting and significant. In the background of the ancient feud looms the figure of that god whom the Norsemen called Frey (the Lord) or Yngvi-frey, and the Angles called Ing: a god of the ancient Northern mythology (and religion) of Fertility and Corn. The enmity of the royal houses was connected with the sacred site of a cult of that religion. Ingeld and his father bear names belonging to it. Freawaru herself is named "Protection of the Lord (of Frey)." Yet one of the chief things told later (in Old Icelandic) about Frey is the story in which he falls in love from afar with the daughter of the enemies of the gods, Gerdr, daughter of the giant Gymir, and weds her. Does this prove that Ingeld and Freawaru, or their love, are "merely mythical"? I think not. History often resembles "Myth," because they are both ultimately of the same stuff. If indeed Ingeld and Freawaru never lived, or at least never loved, then it is ultimately from nameless man and woman that they get their tale, or rather into whose tale they have entered. They have been put into the Cauldron, where so many potent things lie simmering agelong on the fire, among them Love-at-first-sight. So too of the god. If no young man had ever fallen in love by chance meeting with a maiden, and found old enmities to stand between him and his love, then the god Frey would never have seen Gerdr the giant's daughter from the high-seat of Odin. But if we speak of a Cauldron, we must not wholly forget the Cooks. There are many things in the Cauldron, but the Cooks do not dip in the ladle quite blindly. Their selection is important. The gods are after all gods, and it is a matter of some moment what stories are told of them. So we must freely admit that a tale of love is more likely to be told of a prince in history, indeed is more likely actually to happen in an historical family whose traditions are those of Golden Frey and the Vanir, rather than those of Odin the Goth, the Necromancer, glutter of the crows, Lord of the Slain. Small wonder that *spell* means both a story told, and a formula of power over living men.

But when we have done all that research — collection and comparison of the tales of many lands — can do; when we have explained many of the elements commonly found embedded in fairy-stories (such as stepmothers, enchanted bears and bulls, cannibal witches, taboos on names, and the like) as relics of ancient customs once practised in daily life, or of beliefs once held as beliefs and not as "fancies" — there remains still a point too often forgotten: that is the effect produced *now* by these old things in the stories as they are.

For one thing they are now *old*, and antiquity has an appeal in itself. The beauty and horror of *The Juniper Tree* (*Von dem Machandelboom*), with its exquisite and tragic beginning, the abominable cannibal stew, the gruesome bones, the gay and vengeful bird-spirit coming out of a mist that rose from the tree, has remained with me since childhood; and yet always the chief flavour of that tale lingering in the memory was not beauty or horror, but distance and a great abyss of time, not measurable even by *twe tusend Johr*. Without the stew and the bones — which children are now too often spared in mollified versions of Grimm[18] — that vision would largely have been lost. I do not think I was

[18] They should not be spared it — unless they are spared the whole story until their digestions are stronger.

harmed by the horror *in the fairy-tale setting*, out of whatever dark beliefs and practices of the past it may have come. Such stories have now a mythical or total (unanalysable) effect, an effect quite independent of the findings of Comparative Folk-lore, and one which it cannot spoil or explain; they open a door on Other Time, and if we pass through, though only for a moment, we stand outside our own time, outside Time itself, maybe.

If we pause, not merely to note that such old elements have been preserved, but to think *how* they have been preserved, we must conclude, I think, that it has happened, often if not always, precisely because of this literary effect. It cannot have been we, or even the brothers Grimm, that first felt it. Fairy-stories are by no means rocky matrices out of which the fossils cannot be prised except by an expert geologist. The ancient elements can be knocked out, or forgotten and dropped out, or replaced by other ingredients with the greatest ease: as any comparison of a story with closely related variants will show. The things that are there must often have been retained (or inserted) because the oral narrators, instinctively or consciously, felt their literary "significance." [19] Even where a prohibition in a fairy-story is guessed to be derived from some taboo once practised long ago, it has probably been preserved in the later stages of the tale's history because of the great mythical significance of prohibition. A sense of that significance may indeed have lain behind some of the taboos themselves. Thou shalt not — or else thou shalt

[19] See Note B at end (p. 76).

depart beggared into endless regret. The gentlest "nursery-tales" know it. Even Peter Rabbit was forbidden a garden, lost his blue coat, and took sick. The Locked Door stands as an eternal Temptation.

CHILDREN

I will now turn to children, and so come to the last and most important of the three questions: what, if any, are the values and functions of fairy-stories *now?* It is usually assumed that children are the natural or the specially appropriate audience for fairy-stories. In describing a fairy-story which they think adults might possibly read for their own entertainment, reviewers frequently indulge in such waggeries as: "this book is for children from the ages of six to sixty." But I have never yet seen the puff of a new motor-model that began thus: "this toy will amuse infants from seventeen to seventy"; though that to my mind would be much more appropriate. Is there any *essential* connexion between children and fairy-stories? Is there any call for comment, if an adult reads them for himself? *Reads* them as tales, that is, not *studies* them as curios. Adults are allowed to collect and study anything, even old theatre programmes or paper bags.

Among those who still have enough wisdom not to think fairy-stories pernicious, the common opinion seems to be that there is a natural connexion between the minds of children and fairy-stories, of the same order as the connexion between children's bodies and milk. I think this is an error; at best an error of false sentiment, and one that is therefore most often made by those who, for whatever private reason (such as child-lessness), tend to think of children as a special kind of creature, almost a different race, rather than as normal, if immature, members of a particular family, and of the human family at large.

Actually, the association of children and fairy-stories is an accident of our domestic history. Fairy-stories have in the modern lettered world been relegated to the "nursery," as shabby or old-fashioned furniture is relegated to the play-room, primarily because the adults do not want it, and do not mind if it is misused.[20] It is not the choice of the children which decides this. Children as a class — except in a common lack of experience they are not one — neither like fairy-stories more, nor understand them better than adults do; and no more than they like many other things. They are young and growing, and normally have keen appetites, so the fairy-stories as a rule go down well enough. But in fact only some children, and some adults, have any special taste for them; and when they have it, it is not exclusive, nor even necessarily dominant.[21] It is a taste, too, that

[20] In the case of stories and other nursery lore, there is also another factor. Wealthier families employed women to look after their children, and the stories were provided by these nurses, who were some-times in touch with rustic and traditional lore forgotten by their "bet-ters." It is long since this source dried up, at any rate in England; but it once had some importance. But again there is no proof of the special fitness of children as the recipients of this vanishing "folk-lore." The nurses might just as well (or better) have been left to choose the pictures and furniture.

[21] See Note C at end (p. 77).

would not appear, I think, very early in childhood without artificial stimulus; it is certainly one that does not decrease but increases with age, if it is innate.

It is true that in recent times fairy-stories have usually been written or "adapted" for children. But so may music be, or verse, or novels, or history, or scientific manuals. It is a dangerous process, even when it is necessary. It is indeed only saved from disaster by the fact that the arts and sciences are not as a whole relegated to the nursery; the nursery and schoolroom are merely given such tastes and glimpses of the adult thing as seem fit for them in adult opinion (often much mistaken). Any one of these things would, if left altogether in the nursery, become gravely impaired. So would a beautiful table, a good picture, or a useful machine (such as a microscope), be defaced or broken, if it were left long unregarded in a schoolroom. Fairy-stories banished in this way, cut off from a full adult art, would in the end be ruined; indeed in so far as they have been so banished, they have been ruined.

The value of fairy-stories is thus not, in my opinion, to be found by considering children in particular. Collections of fairy-stories are, in fact, by nature attics and lumber-rooms, only by temporary and local custom play-rooms. Their contents are disordered, and often battered, a jumble of different dates, purposes, and tastes; but among them may occasionally be found a thing of permanent virtue: an old work of art, not too much damaged, that only stupidity would ever have stuffed away.

Andrew Lang's *Fairy Books* are not, perhaps, lumber-rooms. They are more like stalls in a rummage-sale. Someone with a duster and a fair eye for things that retain some value has been round the attics and box-rooms. His collections are largely a by-product of his adult study of mythology and folk-lore; but they were made into and presented as books for children.[22] Some of the reasons that Lang gave are worth considering.

The introduction to the first of the series speaks of "children to whom and for whom they are told." "They represent," he says, "the young age of man true to his early loves, and have his unblunted edge of belief, a fresh appetite for marvels." " 'Is it true?' " he says, "is the great question children ask."

I suspect that *belief* and *appetite for marvels* are here regarded as identical or as closely related. They are radically different, though the appetite for marvels is not at once or at first differentiated by a growing human mind from its general appetite. It seems fairly clear that Lang was using *belief* in its ordinary sense: belief that a thing exists or can happen in the real (primary) world. If so, then I fear that Lang's words, stripped of sentiment, can only imply that the teller of marvellous tales to children must, or may, or at any rate does trade on their *credulity*, on the lack of experience which makes it less easy for children to distinguish fact from fiction in particular cases, though the distinction in itself is fundamental to the sane human mind, and to fairy-stories.

Children are capable, of course, of *literary belief*,

[22] By Lang and his helpers. It is not true of the majority of the contents in their original (or oldest surviving) forms.

when the story-maker's art is good enough to produce it. That state of mind has been called "willing suspension of disbelief." But this does not seem to me a good description of what happens. What really happens is that the story-maker proves a successful "sub-creator." He makes a Secondary World which your mind can enter. Inside it, what he relates is "true": it accords with the laws of that world. You therefore believe it, while you are, as it were, inside. The moment disbelief arises, the spell is broken; the magic, or rather art, has failed. You are then out in the Primary World again, looking at the little abortive Secondary World from outside. If you are obliged, by kindliness or circumstance, to stay, then disbelief must be suspended (or stifled), otherwise listening and looking would become intolerable. But this suspension of disbelief is a substitute for the genuine thing, a subterfuge we use when condescending to games or make-believe, or when trying (more or less willingly) to find what virtue we can in the work of an art that has for us failed.

A real enthusiast for cricket is in the enchanted state: Secondary Belief. I, when I watch a match, am on the lower level. I can achieve (more or less) willing suspension of disbelief, when I am held there and supported by some other motive that will keep away boredom: for instance, a wild, heraldic, preference for dark blue rather than light. This suspension of disbelief may thus be a somewhat tired, shabby, or sentimental state of mind, and so lean to the "adult." I fancy it is often the state of adults in the presence of a fairy-story. They are held there and supported by sentiment (memories of childhood, or notions of what childhood ought to be like); they think they ought to like the tale. But if they really liked it, for itself, they would not have to suspend disbelief: they would believe — in this sense.

Now if Lang had meant anything like this there might have been some truth in his words. It may be argued that it is easier to work the spell with children. Perhaps it is, though I am not sure of this. The appearance that it is so is often, I think, an adult illusion produced by children's humility, their lack of critical experience and vocabulary, and their voracity (proper to their rapid growth). They like or try to like what is given to them: if they do not like it, they cannot well express their dislike or give reasons for it (and so may conceal it); and they like a great mass of different things indiscriminately, without troubling to analyse the planes of their belief. In any case I doubt if this potion — the enchantment of the effective fairy-story — is really one of the kind that becomes "blunted" by use, less potent after repeated draughts.

" 'Is it true?' is the great question children ask," Lang said. They do ask that question, I know; and it is not one to be rashly or idly answered.[23] But that question is hardly evidence of "unblunted belief," or even of the desire for it. Most often it proceeds from the child's desire to know which kind of literature he is faced with. Children's knowledge of the world is often so small that they cannot judge, off-hand and without help, between

[23] Far more often they have asked me: "Was he good? Was he wicked?" That is, they were more concerned to get the Right side and the Wrong side clear. For that is a question equally important in History and in Faërie.

the fantastic, the strange (that is rare or remote facts), the nonsensical, and the merely "grown-up" (that is ordinary things of their parents' world, much of which still remains unexplored). But they recognize the different classes, and may like all of them at times. Of course the borders between them are often fluctuating or confused; but that is not only true for children. We all know the differences in kind, but we are not always sure how to place anything that we hear. A child may well believe a report that there are ogres in the next county; many grown-up persons find it easy to believe of another country; and as for another planet, very few adults seem able to imagine it as peopled, if at all, by anything but monsters of iniquity.

Now I was one of the children whom Andrew Lang was addressing — I was born at about the same time as the *Green Fairy Book* — the children for whom he seemed to think that fairy-stories were the equivalent of the adult novel, and of whom he said: "Their taste remains like the taste of their naked ancestors thousands of years ago; and they seem to like fairy-tales better than history, poetry, geography, or arithmetic." [24] But do we really know much about these "naked ancestors," except that they were certainly not naked? Our fairy-stories, however old certain elements in them may be, are certainly not the same as theirs. Yet if it is assumed that we have fairy-stories because they did, then probably we have history, geography, poetry, and arithmetic because they liked these things too, as far as they could get them, and in so far as they had yet separated the

[24] Preface to the *Violet Fairy Book*.

many branches of their general interest in everything.

And as for children of the present day, Lang's description does not fit my own memories, or my experience of children. Lang may have been mistaken about the children he knew, but if he was not, then at any rate children differ considerably, even within the narrow borders of Britain, and such generalizations which treat them as a class (disregarding their individual talents, and the influences of the countryside they live in, and their upbringing) are delusory. I had no special "wish to believe." I wanted to know. Belief depended on the way in which stories were presented to me, by older people, or by the authors, or on the inherent tone and quality of the tale. But at no time can I remember that the enjoyment of a story was dependent on belief that such things could happen, or had happened, in "real life." Fairy-stories were plainly not primarily concerned with possibility, but with desirability. If they awakened *desire*, satisfying it while often whetting it unbearably, they succeeded. It is not necessary to be more explicit here, for I hope to say something later about this desire, a complex of many ingredients, some universal, some particular to modern men (including modern children), or even to certain kinds of men. I had no desire to have either dreams or adventures like *Alice*, and the account of them merely amused me. I had very little desire to look for buried treasure or fight pirates, and *Treasure Island* left me cool. Red Indians were better: there were bows and arrows (I had and have a wholly unsatisfied desire to shoot well with a bow), and strange languages, and glimpses of an ar-

chaic mode of life, and, above all, forests in such stories.
But the land of Merlin and Arthur was better than
these, and best of all the nameless North of Sigurd of
the Völsungs, and the prince of all dragons. Such lands
were pre-eminently desirable. I never imagined that
the dragon was of the same order as the horse. And that
was not solely because I saw horses daily, but never
even the footprint of a worm.[25] The dragon had the
trade-mark *Of Faërie* written plain upon him. In whatever world he had his being it was an Other-world.
Fantasy, the making or glimpsing of Other-worlds, was
the heart of the desire of Faërie. I desired dragons with
a profound desire. Of course, I in my timid body did
not wish to have them in the neighbourhood, intruding
into my relatively safe world, in which it was, for instance, possible to read stories in peace of mind, free
from fear.[26] But the world that contained even the imagination of Fáfnir was richer and more beautiful, at
whatever cost of peril. The dweller in the quiet and
fertile plains may hear of the tormented hills and the
unharvested sea and long for them in his heart. For the
heart is hard though the body be soft.

All the same, important as I now perceive the fairy-
story element in early reading to have been, speaking
for myself as a child, I can only say that a liking for
fairy-stories was not a dominant characteristic of early
taste. A real taste for them awoke after "nursery" days,

[25] See Note D at end (p. 78).
[26] This is, naturally, often enough what children mean when they
ask: "Is it true?" They mean: "I like this, but is it contemporary? Am
I safe in my bed?" The answer: "There is certainly no dragon in England today," is all that they want to hear.

and after the years, few but long-seeming, between learning to read and going to school. In that (I nearly wrote "happy" or "golden," it was really a sad and troublous) time I liked many other things as well, or better: such as history, astronomy, botany, grammar, and etymology. I agreed with Lang's generalized "children" not at all in principle, and only in some points by accident: I was, for instance, insensitive to poetry, and skipped it if it came in tales. Poetry I discovered much later in Latin and Greek, and especially through being made to try and translate English verse into classical verse. A real taste for fairy-stories was wakened by philology on the threshold of manhood, and quickened to full life by war.

I have said, perhaps, more than enough on this point. At least it will be plain that in my opinion fairy-stories should not be *specially* associated with children. They are associated with them: naturally, because children are human and fairy-stories are a natural human taste (though not necessarily a universal one); accidentally, because fairy-stories are a large part of the literary lumber that in latter-day Europe has been stuffed away in attics; unnaturally, because of erroneous sentiment about children, a sentiment that seems to increase with the decline in children.

It is true that the age of childhood-sentiment has produced some delightful books (especially charming, however, to adults) of the fairy kind or near to it; but it has also produced a dreadful undergrowth of stories written or adapted to what was or is conceived to be the measure of children's minds and needs. The old stories are mollified or bowdlerized, instead of being reserved; the imitations are often merely silly, Pigwiggenry without even the intrigue; or patronizing; or (deadliest of all) covertly sniggering, with an eye on the other grown-ups present. I will not accuse Andrew Lang of sniggering, but certainly he smiled to himself, and certainly too often he had an eye on the faces of other clever people over the heads of his child-audience — to the very grave detriment of the *Chronicles of Pantouflia*.

Dasent replied with vigour and justice to the prudish critics of his translations from Norse popular tales. Yet he committed the astonishing folly of particularly *forbidding* children to read the last two in his collection. That a man could study fairy-stories and not learn better than that seems almost incredible. But neither criticism, rejoinder, nor prohibition would have been necessary if children had not unnecessarily been regarded as the inevitable readers of the book.

I do not deny that there is a truth in Andrew Lang's words (sentimental though they may sound): "He who would enter into the Kingdom of Faërie should have the heart of a little child." For that possession is necessary to all high adventure, into kingdoms both less and far greater than Faërie. But humility and innocence — these things "the heart of a child" must mean in such a context — do not necessarily imply an uncritical wonder, nor indeed an uncritical tenderness. Chesterton once remarked that the children in whose company he saw Maeterlinck's *Blue Bird* were dissatisfied "because it did not end with a Day of Judgement, and it was not revealed to the hero and the heroine that the Dog had been faithful and the Cat faithless." "For children," he says, "are innocent and love justice; while most of us are wicked and naturally prefer mercy."

Andrew Lang was confused on this point. He was at pains to defend the slaying of the Yellow Dwarf by Prince Ricardo in one of his own fairy-stories. "I hate cruelty," he said, ". . . but that was in fair fight, sword in hand, and the dwarf, peace to his ashes! died in harness." Yet it is not clear that "fair fight" is less cruel than "fair judgement"; or that piercing a dwarf with a sword is more just than the execution of wicked kings and evil stepmothers — which Lang abjures: he sends the criminals (as he boasts) to retirement on ample pensions. That is mercy untempered by justice. It is true that this plea was not addressed to children but to parents and guardians, to whom Lang was recommending his own *Prince Prigio* and *Prince Ricardo* as suitable for their charges.[27] It is parents and guardians who have classified fairy-stories as *Juvenilia*. And this is a small sample of the falsification of values that results.

If we use *child* in a good sense (it has also legitimately a bad one) we must not allow that to push us into the sentimentality of only using *adult* or *grown-up* in a bad sense (it has also legitimately a good one). The process of growing older is not necessarily allied to growing wickeder, though the two do often happen together. Children are meant to grow up, and not to become Peter Pans. Not to lose innocence and wonder, but to proceed on the appointed journey: that journey

[27] Preface to the *Lilac Fairy Book.*

upon which it is certainly not better to travel hopefully
than to arrive, though we must travel hopefully if we are
to arrive. But it is one of the lessons of fairy-stories (if
we can speak of the lessons of things that do not lecture) that on callow, lumpish, and selfish youth peril,
sorrow, and the shadow of death can bestow dignity,
and even sometimes wisdom.

Let us not divide the human race into Eloi and Morlocks: pretty children — "elves" as the eighteenth century often idiotically called them — with their fairy-
tales (carefully pruned), and dark Morlocks tending
their machines. If fairy-story as a kind is worth reading
at all it is worthy to be written for and read by adults.
They will, of course, put more in and get more out than
children can. Then, as a branch of a genuine art, children may hope to get fairy-stories fit for them to read
and yet within their measure; as they may hope to get
suitable introductions to poetry, history, and the sciences. Though it may be better for them to read some
things, especially fairy-stories, that are beyond their
measure rather than short of it. Their books like their
clothes should allow for growth, and their books at any
rate should encourage it.

Very well, then. If adults are to read fairy-stories as a
natural branch of literature — neither playing at being
children, nor pretending to be choosing for children,
nor being boys who would not grow up — what are the
values and functions of this kind? That is, I think, the
last and most important question. I have already
hinted at some of my answers. First of all: if written
with art, the prime value of fairy-stories will simply be

that value which, as literature, they share with other literary forms. But fairy-stories offer also, in a peculiar degree or mode, these things: Fantasy, Recovery, Escape, Consolation, all things of which children have, as a rule, less need than older people. Most of them are nowadays very commonly considered to be bad for anybody. I will consider them briefly, and will begin with *Fantasy*.

## FANTASY

The human mind is capable of forming mental images of things not actually present. The faculty of conceiving the images is (or was) naturally called Imagination. But in recent times, in technical not normal language, Imagination has often been held to be something higher than the mere image-making, ascribed to the operations of Fancy (a reduced and depreciatory form of the older word Fantasy); an attempt is thus made to restrict, I should say misapply, Imagination to "the power of giving to ideal creations the inner consistency of reality."

Ridiculous though it may be for one so ill-instructed to have an opinion on this critical matter, I venture to think the verbal distinction philologically inappropriate, and the analysis inaccurate. The mental power of image-making is one thing, or aspect; and it should appropriately be called Imagination. The perception of the image, the grasp of its implications, and the control,

which are necessary to a successful expression, may
vary in vividness and strength: but this is a difference
of degree in Imagination, not a difference in kind. The
achievement of the expression, which gives (or seems to
give) "the inner consistency of reality," [28] is indeed another thing, or aspect, needing another name: Art, the
operative link between Imagination and the final result,
Sub-creation. For my present purpose I require a word
which shall embrace both the Sub-creative Art in itself
and a quality of strangeness and wonder in the Expression, derived from the Image: a quality essential to
fairy-story. I propose, therefore, to arrogate to myself
the powers of Humpty-Dumpty, and to use Fantasy for
this purpose: in a sense, that is, which combines with its
older and higher use as an equivalent of Imagination the
derived notions of "unreality" (that is, of unlikeness to
the Primary World), of freedom from the domination
of observed "fact," in short of the fantastic. I am thus
not only aware but glad of the etymological and seman-
tic connexions of *fantasy* with *fantastic*: with images of
things that are not only "not actually present," but which
are indeed not to be found in our primary world at
all, or are generally believed not to be found there. But
while admitting that, I do not assent to the depreciative
tone. That the images are of things not in the primary
world (if that indeed is possible) is a virtue, not a vice.
Fantasy (in this sense) is, I think, not a lower but a
higher form of Art, indeed the most nearly pure form,
and so (when achieved) the most potent.

Fantasy, of course, starts out with an advantage: ar-

[28] That is: which commands or induces Secondary Belief.

resting strangeness. But that advantage has been turned against it, and has contributed to its disrepute. Many people dislike being "arrested." They dislike any meddling with the Primary World, or such small glimpses of it as are familiar to them. They, therefore, stupidly and even maliciously confound Fantasy with Dreaming, in which there is no Art;[29] and with mental disorders, in which there is not even control: with delusion and hallucination.

But the error or malice, engendered by disquiet and consequent dislike, is not the only cause of this confusion. Fantasy has also an essential drawback: it is difficult to achieve. Fantasy may be, as I think, not less but more sub-creative; but at any rate it is found in practice that "the inner consistency of reality" is more difficult to produce, the more unlike are the images and the rearrangements of primary material to the actual arrangements of the Primary World. It is easier to produce this kind of "reality" with more "sober" material. Fantasy thus, too often, remains undeveloped; it is and has been used frivolously, or only half-seriously, or merely for decoration: it remains merely "fanciful." Anyone inheriting the fantastic device of human language can say *the green sun*. Many can then imagine or picture it. But that is not enough — though it may already be a more potent thing than many a "thumbnail sketch" or "transcript of life" that receives literary praise.

To make a Secondary World inside which the green

[29] This is not true of all dreams. In some Fantasy seems to take a part. But this is exceptional. Fantasy is a rational, not an irrational, activity.

sun will be credible, commanding Secondary Belief, will probably require labour and thought, and will certainly demand a special skill, a kind of elvish craft. Few attempt such difficult tasks. But when they are attempted and in any degree accomplished then we have a rare achievement of Art: indeed narrative art, story-making in its primary and most potent mode.

In human art Fantasy is a thing best left to words, to true literature. In painting, for instance, the visible presentation of the fantastic image is technically too easy; the hand tends to outrun the mind, even to overthrow it.[30] Silliness or morbidity are frequent results. It is a misfortune that Drama, an art fundamentally distinct from Literature, should so commonly be considered together with it, or as a branch of it. Among these misfortunes we may reckon the depreciation of Fantasy. For in part at least this depreciation is due to the natural desire of critics to cry up the forms of literature or "imagination" that they themselves, innately or by training, prefer. And criticism in a country that has produced so great a Drama, and possesses the works of William Shakespeare, tends to be far too dramatic. But Drama is naturally hostile to Fantasy. Fantasy, even of the simplest kind, hardly ever succeeds in Drama, when that is presented as it should be, visibly and audibly acted. Fantastic forms are not to be counterfeited. Men dressed up as talking animals may achieve buffoonery or mimicry, but they do not achieve Fantasy. This is, I think, well illustrated by the failure of the bastard form, pantomime. The nearer it is to "dramatized

[30] See Note E at end (p. 79).

fairy-story" the worse it is. It is only tolerable when the
plot and its fantasy are reduced to a mere vestigiary
framework for farce, and no "belief" of any kind in any
part of the performance is required or expected of anybody. This is, of course, partly due to the fact that the
producers of drama have to, or try to, work with mechanism to represent either Fantasy or Magic. I once saw
a so-called "children's pantomime," the straight story of
*Puss-in-Boots*, with even the metamorphosis of the ogre
into a mouse. Had this been mechanically successful it
would either have terrified the spectators or else have
been just a turn of high-class conjuring. As it was,
though done with some ingenuity of lighting, disbelief
had not so much to be suspended as hanged, drawn, and
quartered.

In *Macbeth*, when it is read, I find the witches tolerable: they have a narrative function and some hint of
dark significance; though they are vulgarized, poor
things of their kind. They are almost intolerable in the
play. They would be quite intolerable, if I were not for-
tified by some memory of them as they are in the story
as read. I am told that I should feel differently if I had
the mind of the period, with its witch-hunts and witch-
trials. But that is to say: if I regarded the witches as
possible, indeed likely, in the Primary World; in other
words, if they ceased to be "Fantasy." That argument
concedes the point. To be dissolved, or to be degraded,
is the likely fate of Fantasy when a dramatist tries to use
it, even such a dramatist as Shakespeare. *Macbeth* is indeed a work by a playwright who ought, at least on this
occasion, to have written a story, if he had the skill or
patience for that art.

A reason, more important, I think, than the inadequacy of stage-effects, is this: Drama has, of its very nature, already attempted a kind of bogus, or shall I say at least substitute, magic: *the visible and audible presentation of imaginary men in a story*. That is in itself an attempt to counterfeit the magician's wand. To introduce, even with mechanical success, into this quasi-magical secondary world a further fantasy or magic is to demand, as it were, an inner or tertiary world. It is a world too much. To make such a thing may not be impossible. I have never seen it done with success. But at least it cannot be claimed as the proper mode of Drama, in which walking and talking people have been found to be the natural instruments of Art and illusion.[31]

For this precise reason — that the characters, and even the scenes, are in Drama not imagined but actually beheld — Drama is, even though it uses a similar material (words, verse, plot), an art fundamentally different from narrative art. Thus, if you prefer Drama to Literature (as many literary critics plainly do), or form your critical theories primarily from dramatic critics, or even from Drama, you are apt to misunderstand pure story-making, and to constrain it to the limitations of stage-plays. You are, for instance, likely to prefer characters, even the basest and dullest, to things. Very little about trees as trees can be got into a play.

Now "Faërian Drama" — those plays which according to abundant records the elves have often presented to men — can produce Fantasy with a realism and immediacy beyond the compass of any human mechanism. As a result their usual effect (upon a man) is to go be-

[31] See Note F at end (p. 80).

yond Secondary Belief. If you are present at a Faërian drama you yourself are, or think that you are, bodily inside its Secondary World. The experience may be very similar to Dreaming and has (it would seem) sometimes (by men) been confounded with it. But in Faërian drama you are in a dream that some other mind is weaving, and the knowledge of that alarming fact may slip from your grasp. To experience *directly* a Secondary World: the potion is too strong, and you give to it Primary Belief, however marvellous the events. You are deluded — whether that is the intention of the elves (always or at any time) is another question. They at any rate are not themselves deluded. This is for them a form of Art, and distinct from Wizardry or Magic, properly so called. They do not live in it, though they can, perhaps, afford to spend more time at it than human artists can. The Primary World, Reality, of elves and men is the same, if differently valued and perceived.

We need a word for this elvish craft, but all the words that have been applied to it have been blurred and confused with other things. Magic is ready to hand, and I have used it above (p. 10), but I should not have done so: Magic should be reserved for the operations of the Magician. Art is the human process that produces by the way (it is not its only or ultimate object) Secondary Belief. Art of the same sort, if more skilled and effortless, the elves can also use, or so the reports seem to show; but the more potent and specially elvish craft I will, for lack of a less debatable word, call Enchantment. Enchantment produces a Secondary World into which both designer and spectator can enter, to the satisfaction of their senses while they are inside; but in its purity it is artistic in desire and purpose. Magic produces, or pretends to produce, an alteration in the Primary World. It does not matter by whom it is said to be practised, fay or mortal, it remains distinct from the other two; it is not an art but a technique; its desire is *power* in this world, domination of things and wills.

To the elvish craft, Enchantment, Fantasy aspires, and when it is successful of all forms of human art most nearly approaches. At the heart of many man-made stories of the elves lies, open or concealed, pure or alloyed, the desire for a living, realized sub-creative art, which (however much it may outwardly resemble it) is inwardly wholly different from the greed for self-centred power which is the mark of the mere Magician. Of this desire the elves, in their better (but still perilous) part, are largely made; and it is from them that we may learn what is the central desire and aspiration of human Fantasy — even if the elves are, all the more in so far as they are, only a product of Fantasy itself. That creative desire is only cheated by counterfeits, whether the innocent but clumsy devices of the human dramatist, or the malevolent frauds of the magicians. In this world it is for men unsatisfiable, and so imperishable. Uncorrupted, it does not seek delusion nor bewitchment and domination; it seeks shared enrichment, partners in making and delight, not slaves.

To many, Fantasy, this sub-creative art which plays strange tricks with the world and all that is in it, combining nouns and redistributing adjectives, has seemed suspect, if not illegitimate. To some it has seemed at least a childish folly, a thing only for peoples or for persons in their youth. As for its legitimacy I will say no more than to quote a brief passage from a letter I once wrote to a man who described myth and fairy-story as "lies"; though to do him justice he was kind enough and confused enough to call fairy-story-making "Breathing a lie through Silver."

> *"Dear Sir,"* I said — *"Although now long estranged,*
> *Man is not wholly lost nor wholly changed.*
> *Dis-graced he may be, yet is not de-throned,*
> *and keeps the rags of lordship once he owned:*
> *Man, Sub-creator, the refracted Light*
> *through whom is splintered from a single White*
> *to many hues, and endlessly combined*
> *in living shapes that move from mind to mind.*
> *Though all the crannies of the world we filled*
> *with Elves and Goblins, though we dared to build*
> *Gods and their houses out of dark and light,*
> *and sowed the seed of dragons — 'twas our right*
> *(used or misused). That right has not decayed:*
> *we make still by the law in which we're made."*

Fantasy is a natural human activity. It certainly does not destroy or even insult Reason; and it does not either blunt the appetite for, nor obscure the perception of, scientific verity. On the contrary. The keener and the clearer is the reason, the better fantasy will it make. If men were ever in a state in which they did not want to know or could not perceive truth (facts or evidence), then Fantasy would languish until they were cured. If they ever get into that state (it would not seem at all impossible), Fantasy will perish, and become Morbid Delusion.

For creative Fantasy is founded upon the hard recognition that things are so in the world as it appears under the sun; on a recognition of fact, but not a slavery to it. So upon logic was founded the nonsense that displays itself in the tales and rhymes of Lewis Carroll. If men really could not distinguish between frogs and men, fairy-stories about frog-kings would not have arisen.

Fantasy can, of course, be carried to excess. It can be ill done. It can be put to evil uses. It may even delude the minds out of which it came. But of what human thing in this fallen world is that not true? Men have conceived not only of elves, but they have imagined gods, and worshipped them, even worshipped those most deformed by their authors' own evil. But they have made false gods out of other materials: their notions, their banners, their monies; even their sciences and their social and economic theories have demanded human sacrifice. *Abusus non tollit usum.* Fantasy remains a human right: we make in our measure and in our derivative mode, because we are made: and not only made, but made in the image and likeness of a Maker.

## RECOVERY, ESCAPE, CONSOLATION

As for old age, whether personal or belonging to the times in which we live, it may be true, as is often sup-

posed, that this imposes disabilities (cf. p. 35). But it is
in the main an idea produced by the mere *study* of
fairy-stories. The analytic study of fairy-stories is as
bad a preparation for the enjoying or the writing of
them as would be the historical study of the drama
of all lands and times for the enjoyment or writing of
stage-plays. The study may indeed become depressing.
It is easy for the student to feel that with all his labour
he is collecting only a few leaves, many of them now
torn or decayed, from the countless foliage of the Tree
of Tales, with which the Forest of Days is carpeted. It
seems vain to add to the litter. Who can design a new
leaf? The patterns from bud to unfolding, and the colours from spring to autumn were all discovered by men
long ago. But that is not true. The seed of the tree can
be replanted in almost any soil, even in one so smoke-
ridden (as Lang said) as that of England. Spring is, of
course, not really less beautiful because we have seen or
heard of other like events: like events, never from
world's beginning to world's end the same event. Each
leaf, of oak and ash and thorn, is a unique embodiment
of the pattern, and for some this very year may be *the*
embodiment, the first ever seen and recognized, though
oaks have put forth leaves for countless generations of
men.

We do not, or need not, despair of drawing because
all lines must be either curved or straight, nor of painting because there are only three "primary" colours. We
may indeed be older now, in so far as we are heirs in enjoyment or in practice of many generations of ancestors
in the arts. In this inheritance of wealth there may be a

danger of boredom or of anxiety to be original, and that
may lead to a distaste for fine drawing, delicate pattern,
and "pretty" colours, or else to mere manipulation and
over-elaboration of old material, clever and heartless.
But the true road of escape from such weariness is not
to be found in the wilfully awkward, clumsy, or mis-
shapen, not in making all things dark or unremittingly
violent; nor in the mixing of colours on through sub-
tlety to drabness, and the fantastical complication of
shapes to the point of silliness and on towards delir-
ium. Before we reach such states we need recovery.
We should look at green again, and be startled anew
(but not blinded) by blue and yellow and red. We
should meet the centaur and the dragon, and then perhaps suddenly behold, like the ancient shepherds,
sheep, and dogs, and horses — and wolves. This recovery fairy-stories help us to make. In that sense only a
taste for them may make us, or keep us, childish.

Recovery (which includes return and renewal of
health) is a re-gaining — regaining of a clear view. I
do not say "seeing things as they are" and involve myself
with the philosophers, though I might venture to say
"seeing things as we are (or were) meant to see them"
— as things apart from ourselves. We need, in any
case, to clean our windows; so that the things seen
clearly may be freed from the drab blur of triteness or
familiarity — from possessiveness. Of all faces those of
our *familiares* are the ones both most difficult to play
fantastic tricks with, and most difficult really to see with
fresh attention, perceiving their likeness and unlikeness: that they are faces, and yet unique faces. This

triteness is really the penalty of "appropriation": the things that are trite, or (in a bad sense) familiar, are the things that we have appropriated, legally or mentally. We say we know them. They have become like the things which once attracted us by their glitter, or their colour, or their shape, and we laid hands on them, and then locked them in our hoard, acquired them, and acquiring ceased to look at them.

Of course, fairy-stories are not the only means of recovery, or prophylactic against loss. Humility is enough. And there is (especially for the humble) *Mooreeffoc*, or Chestertonian Fantasy. *Mooreeffoc* is a fantastic word, but it could be seen written up in every town in this land. It is Coffee-room, viewed from the inside through a glass door, as it was seen by Dickens on a dark London day; and it was used by Chesterton to denote the queerness of things that have become trite, when they are seen suddenly from a new angle. That kind of "fantasy" most people would allow to be wholesome enough; and it can never lack for material. But it has, I think, only a limited power; for the reason that recovery of freshness of vision is its only virtue. The word *Mooreeffoc* may cause you suddenly to realize that England is an utterly alien land, lost either in some remote past age glimpsed by history, or in some strange dim future to be reached only by a time-machine; to see the amazing oddity and interest of its inhabitants and their customs and feeding-habits; but it cannot do more than that: act as a time-telescope focused on one spot. Creative fantasy, because it is mainly trying to do something else (make something new), may open your hoard and let all the locked things fly away like cage-birds. The gems all turn into flowers or flames, and you will be warned that all you had (or knew) was dangerous and potent, not really effectively chained, free and wild; no more yours than they were you.

The "fantastic" elements in verse and prose of other kinds, even when only decorative or occasional, help in this release. But not so thoroughly as a fairy-story, a thing built on or about Fantasy, of which Fantasy is the core. Fantasy is made out of the Primary World, but a good craftsman loves his material, and has a knowledge and feeling for clay, stone and wood which only the art of making can give. By the forging of Gram cold iron was revealed; by the making of Pegasus horses were ennobled; in the Trees of the Sun and Moon root and stock, flower and fruit are manifested in glory.

And actually fairy-stories deal largely, or (the better ones) mainly, with simple or fundamental things, untouched by Fantasy, but these simplicities are made all the more luminous by their setting. For the story-maker who allows himself to be "free with" Nature can be her lover not her slave. It was in fairy-stories that I first divined the potency of the words, and the wonder of the things, such as stone, and wood, and iron; tree and grass; house and fire; bread and wine.

I will now conclude by considering Escape and Consolation, which are naturally closely connected. Though fairy-stories are of course by no means the only medium of Escape, they are today one of the most obvious and (to some) outrageous forms of "escapist" literature; and it is thus reasonable to attach to a consideration of them some considerations of this term "escape" in criticism generally.

I have claimed that Escape is one of the main functions of fairy-stories, and since I do not disapprove of them, it is plain that I do not accept the tone of scorn or pity with which "Escape" is now so often used: a tone for which the uses of the word outside literary criticism give no warrant at all. In what the misusers are fond of calling Real Life, Escape is evidently as a rule very practical, and may even be heroic. In real life it is difficult to blame it, unless it fails; in criticism it would seem to be the worse the better it succeeds. Evidently we are faced by a misuse of words, and also by a confusion of thought. Why should a man be scorned if, finding himself in prison, he tries to get out and go home? Or if, when he cannot do so, he thinks and talks about other topics than jailers and prison-walls? The world outside has not become less real because the prisoner cannot see it. In using Escape in this way the critics have chosen the wrong word, and, what is more, they are confusing, not always by sincere error, the Escape of the Prisoner with the Flight of the Deserter. Just so a Party-spokesman might have labelled departure from the misery of the Führer's or any other Reich and even criticism of it as treachery. In the same way these critics, to make confusion worse, and so to bring into contempt their opponents, stick their label of scorn not only on to Desertion, but on to real Escape, and what are often its companions, Disgust, Anger, Condemnation, and Revolt. Not only do they confound the escape of the prisoner with the flight of the deserter; but they would seem to prefer the acquiescence of the "quisling" to the resistance of the patriot. To such thinking you have only to say "the land you loved is doomed" to excuse any treachery, indeed to glorify it.

For a trifling instance: not to mention (indeed not to parade) electric street-lamps of mass-produced pattern in your tale is Escape (in that sense). But it may, almost certainly does, proceed from a considered disgust for so typical a product of the Robot Age, that combines elaboration and ingenuity of means with ugliness, and (often) with inferiority of result. These lamps may be excluded from the tale simply because they are bad lamps; and it is possible that one of the lessons to be learnt from the story is the realization of this fact. But out comes the big stick: "Electric lamps have come to stay," they say. Long ago Chesterton truly remarked that, as soon as he heard that anything "had come to stay," he knew that it would be very soon replaced — indeed regarded as pitiably obsolete and shabby. "The march of Science, its tempo quickened by the needs of war, goes inexorably on . . . making some things obsolete, and foreshadowing new developments in the utilization of electricity": an advertisement. This says the same thing only more menacingly. The electric street-lamp may indeed be ignored, simply because it is so insignificant and transient. Fairy-stories, at any rate, have many more permanent and fundamental things to talk about. Lightning, for example. The escapist is not so subservient to the whims of evanescent fashion as these opponents. He does not make things (which it may be quite rational to regard as bad) his masters or his gods by worshipping them as inevitable, even "inexorable." And his opponents, so easily contemptuous, have no guarantee that he will stop there: he might rouse men to pull down the street-lamps. Escapism has another and even wickeder face: Reaction.

Not long ago — incredible though it may seem — I heard a clerk of Oxenford declare that he "welcomed" the proximity of mass-production robot factories, and the roar of self-obstructive mechanical traffic, because it brought his university into "contact with real life." He may have meant that the way men were living and working in the twentieth century was increasing in barbarity at an alarming rate, and that the loud demonstration of this in the streets of Oxford might serve as a warning that it is not possible to preserve for long an oasis of sanity in a desert of unreason by mere fences, without actual offensive action (practical and intellectual). I fear he did not. In any case the expression "real life" in this context seems to fall short of academic standards. The notion that motor-cars are more "alive" than, say, centaurs or dragons is curious; that they are more "real" than, say, horses is pathetically absurd. How real, how startlingly alive is a factory chimney compared with an elm-tree: poor obsolete thing, insubstantial dream of an escapist!

For my part, I cannot convince myself that the roof of Bletchley station is more "real" than the clouds. And as an artefact I find it less inspiring than the legendary dome of heaven. The bridge to platform 4 is to me less interesting than Bifröst guarded by Heimdall with the

Gjallarhorn. From the wildness of my heart I cannot exclude the question whether railway-engineers, if they had been brought up on more fantasy, might not have done better with all their abundant means than they commonly do. Fairy-stories might be, I guess, better Masters of Arts than the academic person I have referred to.

Much that he (I must suppose) and others (certainly) would call "serious" literature is no more than play under a glass roof by the side of a municipal swimming-bath. Fairy-stories may invent monsters that fly the air or dwell in the deep, but at least they do not try to escape from heaven or the sea.

And if we leave aside for a moment "fantasy," I do not think that the reader or the maker of fairy-stories need even be ashamed of the "escape" of archaism: of preferring not dragons but horses, castles, sailing-ships, bows and arrows; not only elves, but knights and kings and priests. For it is after all possible for a rational man, after reflection (quite unconnected with fairy-story or romance), to arrive at the condemnation, implicit at least in the mere silence of "escapist" literature, of progressive things like factories, or the machine-guns and bombs that appear to be their most natural and inevitable, dare we say "inexorable," products.

"The rawness and ugliness of modern European life" — that real life whose contact we should welcome — "is the sign of a biological inferiority, of an insufficient or false reaction to environment." [32] The maddest castle

---

[32] Christopher Dawson, *Progress and Religion*, pp. 58, 59. Later he adds: "The full Victorian panoply of top-hat and frock-coat undoubtedly expressed something essential in the nineteenth-century culture,

that ever came out of a giant's bag in a wild Gaelic story is not only much less ugly than a robot-factory, it is also (to use a very modern phrase) "in a very real sense" a great deal more real. Why should we not escape from or condemn the "grim Assyrian" absurdity of top-hats, or the Morlockian horror of factories? They are condemned even by the writers of that most escapist form of all literature, stories of Science fiction. These prophets often foretell (and many seem to yearn for) a world like one big glass-roofed railway-station. But from them it is as a rule very hard to gather what men in such a world-town will *do*. They may abandon the "full Victorian panoply" for loose garments (with zip-fasteners), but will use this freedom mainly, it would appear, in order to play with mechanical toys in the soon-cloying game of moving at high speed. To judge by some of these tales they will still be as lustful, vengeful, and greedy as ever; and the ideals of their idealists hardly reach farther than the splendid notion of building more towns of the same sort on other planets. It is indeed an age of "improved means to deteriorated ends." It is part of the essential malady of such days — producing the desire to escape, not indeed from life, but from our present time and self-made misery — that we are acutely conscious both of the ugliness of our works, and of their

---

and hence it has with that culture spread all over the world, as no fashion of clothing has ever done before. It is possible that our descendants will recognize in it a kind of grim Assyrian beauty, fit emblem of the ruthless and great age that created it; but however that may be, it misses the direct and inevitable beauty that all clothing should have, because like its parent culture it was out of touch with the life of nature and of human nature as well."

evil. So that to us evil and ugliness seem indissolubly allied. We find it difficult to conceive of evil and beauty together. The fear of the beautiful fay that ran through the elder ages almost eludes our grasp. Even more alarming: goodness is itself bereft of its proper beauty. In Faërie one can indeed conceive of an ogre who possesses a castle hideous as a nightmare (for the evil of the ogre wills it so), but one cannot conceive of a house built with a good purpose — an inn, a hostel for travellers, the hall of a virtuous and noble king — that is yet sickeningly ugly. At the present day it would be rash to hope to see one that was not — unless it was built before our time.

This, however, is the modern and special (or accidental) "escapist" aspect of fairy-stories, which they share with romances, and other stories out of or about the past. Many stories out of the past have only become "escapist" in their appeal through surviving from a time when men were as a rule delighted with the work of their hands into our time, when many men feel disgust with man-made things.

But there are also other and more profound "escapisms" that have always appeared in fairy-tale and legend. There are other things more grim and terrible to fly from than the noise, stench, ruthlessness, and extravagance of the internal-combustion engine. There are hunger, thirst, poverty, pain, sorrow, injustice, death. And even when men are not facing hard things such as these, there are ancient limitations from which fairy-stories offer a sort of escape, and old ambitions and desires (touching the very roots of fantasy) to which they offer a kind of satisfaction and consolation. Some are pardonable weaknesses or curiosities: such as the desire to visit, free as a fish, the deep sea; or the longing for the noiseless, gracious, economical flight of a bird, that longing which the aeroplane cheats, except in rare moments, seen high and by wind and distance noiseless, turning in the sun: that is, precisely when imagined and not used. There are profounder wishes: such as the desire to converse with other living things. On this desire, as ancient as the Fall, is largely founded the talking of beasts and creatures in fairy-tales, and especially the magical understanding of their proper speech. This is the root, and not the "confusion" attributed to the minds of men of the unrecorded past, an alleged "absence of the sense of separation of ourselves from beasts." [33] A vivid sense of that separation is very ancient; but also a sense that it was a severance: a strange fate and a guilt lies on us. Other creatures are like other realms with which Man has broken off relations, and sees now only from the outside at a distance, being at war with them, or on the terms of an uneasy armistice. There are a few men who are privileged to travel abroad a little; others must be content with travellers' tales. Even about frogs. In speaking of that rather odd but widespread fairy-story The Frog-King Max Müller asked in his prim way: "How came such a story ever to be invented? Human beings were, we may hope, at all times sufficiently enlightened to know that a marriage between a frog and the daughter of a queen was absurd." Indeed we may hope so! For if not, there would be no point in this

[33] See Note G at end (p. 82).

story at all, depending as it does essentially on the sense of the absurdity. Folk-lore origins (or guesses about them) are here quite beside the point. It is of little avail to consider totemism. For certainly, whatever customs or beliefs about frogs and wells lie behind this story, the frog-shape was and is preserved in the fairy-story[34] precisely because it was so queer and the marriage absurd, indeed abominable. Though, of course, in the versions which concern us, Gaelic, German, English,[35] there is in fact no wedding between a princess and a frog: the frog was an enchanted prince. And the point of the story lies not in thinking frogs possible mates, but in the necessity of keeping promises (even those with intolerable consequences) that, together with observing prohibitions, runs through all Fairyland. This is one of the notes of the horns of Elfland, and not a dim note.

And lastly there is the oldest and deepest desire, the Great Escape: the Escape from Death. Fairy-stories provide many examples and modes of this — which might be called the genuine *escapist*, or (I would say) *fugitive* spirit. But so do other stories (notably those of scientific inspiration), and so do other studies. Fairy-stories are made by men not by fairies. The Human-stories of the elves are doubtless full of the Escape from Deathlessness. But our stories cannot be expected always to rise above our common level. They often do. Few lessons are taught more clearly in them than the

[34] Or group of similar stories.
[35] *The Queen who sought drink from a certain Well and the Lorgann* (Campbell, xxiii); *Der Froschkönig; The Maid and the Frog.*

burden of that kind of immortality, or rather endless serial living, to which the "fugitive" would fly. For the fairy-story is specially apt to teach such things, of old and still today. Death is the theme that most inspired George MacDonald.

But the "consolation" of fairy-tales has another aspect than the imaginative satisfaction of ancient desires. Far more important is the Consolation of the Happy Ending. Almost I would venture to assert that all complete fairy-stories must have it. At least I would say that Tragedy is the true form of Drama, its highest function; but the opposite is true of Fairy-story. Since we do not appear to possess a word that expresses this opposite — I will call it *Eucatastrophe*. The *eucatastrophic* tale is the true form of fairy-tale, and its highest function.

The consolation of fairy-stories, the joy of the happy ending: or more correctly of the good catastrophe, the sudden joyous "turn" (for there is no true end to any fairy-tale): [36] this joy, which is one of the things which fairy-stories can produce supremely well, is not essentially "escapist," nor "fugitive." In its fairy-tale — or otherworld — setting, it is a sudden and miraculous grace: never to be counted on to recur. It does not deny the existence of *dyscatastrophe*, of sorrow and failure: the possibility of these is necessary to the joy of deliverance; it denies (in the face of much evidence, if you will) universal final defeat and in so far is *evangelium*, giving a fleeting glimpse of Joy, Joy beyond the walls of the world, poignant as grief.

It is the mark of a good fairy-story, of the higher or

[36] See Note H at end (p. 83).

more complete kind, that however wild its events, however fantastic or terrible the adventures, it can give to
child or man that hears it, when the "turn" comes, a
catch of the breath, a beat and lifting of the heart, near
to (or indeed accompanied by) tears, as keen as that
given by any form of literary art, and having a peculiar
quality.

Even modern fairy-stories can produce this effect
sometimes. It is not an easy thing to do; it depends on
the whole story which is the setting of the turn, and
yet it reflects a glory backwards. A tale that in any
measure succeeds in this point has not wholly failed,
whatever flaws it may possess, and whatever mixture or
confusion of purpose. It happens even in Andrew
Lang's own fairy-story, *Prince Prigio*, unsatisfactory in
many ways as that is. When "each knight came alive
and lifted his sword and shouted 'long live Prince
Prigio,'" the joy has a little of that strange mythical
fairy-story quality, greater than the event described. It
would have none in Lang's tale, if the event described
were not a piece of more serious fairy-story "fantasy"
than the main bulk of the story, which is in general
more frivolous, having the half-mocking smile of the
courtly, sophisticated *Conte*.[37] Far more powerful and
poignant is the effect in a serious tale of Faërie.[38] In
such stories when the sudden "turn" comes we get a

[37] This is characteristic of Lang's wavering balance. On the surface
the story is a follower of the "courtly" French *conte* with a satirical
twist, and of Thackeray's *Rose and the Ring* in particular — a kind
which being superficial, even frivolous, by nature, does not produce
or aim at producing anything so profound; but underneath lies the
deeper spirit of the romantic Lang.

[38] Of the kind which Lang called "traditional," and really preferred.

piercing glimpse of joy, and heart's desire, that for a moment passes outside the frame, rends indeed the very web of story, and lets a gleam come through.

> "Seven long years I served for thee,
> The glassy hill I clamb for thee,
> The bluidy shirt I wrang for thee,
> And wilt thou not wauken and turn to me?"

He heard and turned to her.[39]


### EPILOGUE

This "joy" which I have selected as the mark of the true fairy-story (or romance), or as the seal upon it, merits more consideration.

Probably every writer making a secondary world, a fantasy, every sub-creator, wishes in some measure to be a real maker, or hopes that he is drawing on reality: hopes that the peculiar quality of this secondary world (if not all the details) [40] are derived from Reality, or are flowing into it. If he indeed achieves a quality that can fairly be described by the dictionary definition: "inner consistency of reality," it is difficult to conceive how this can be, if the work does not in some way partake of reality. The peculiar quality of the "joy" in successful

[39] *The Black Bull of Norroway.*
[40] For all the details may not be "true": it is seldom that the "inspiration" is so strong and lasting that it leavens all the lump, and does not leave much that is mere uninspired "invention."

Fantasy can thus be explained as a sudden glimpse of the underlying reality or truth. It is not only a "consolation" for the sorrow of this world, but a satisfaction, and an answer to that question, "Is it true?" The answer to this question that I gave at first was (quite rightly): "If you have built your little world well, yes: it is true in that world." That is enough for the artist (or the artist part of the artist). But in the "eucatastrophe" we see in a brief vision that the answer may be greater — it may be a far-off gleam or echo of *evangelium* in the real world. The use of this word gives a hint of my epilogue. It is a serious and dangerous matter. It is presumptuous of me to touch upon such a theme; but if by grace what I say has in any respect any validity, it is, of course, only one facet of a truth incalculably rich: finite only because the capacity of Man for whom this was done is finite.

I would venture to say that approaching the Christian Story from this direction, it has long been my feeling (a joyous feeling) that God redeemed the corrupt making-creatures, men, in a way fitting to this aspect, as to others, of their strange nature. The Gospels contain a fairy-story, or a story of a larger kind which embraces all the essence of fairy-stories. They contain many marvels — peculiarly artistic,[41] beautiful, and moving: "mythical" in their perfect, self-contained significance; and among the marvels is the greatest and most complete conceivable eucatastrophe. But this story has entered History and the primary world; the desire and

---

[41] The Art is here in the story itself rather than in the telling; for the Author of the story was not the evangelists.

aspiration of sub-creation has been raised to the fulfilment of Creation. The Birth of Christ is the eucatastrophe of Man's history. The Resurrection is the eucatastrophe of the story of the Incarnation. This story begins and ends in joy. It has pre-eminently the "inner consistency of reality." There is no tale ever told that men would rather find was true, and none which so many sceptical men have accepted as true on its own merits. For the Art of it has the supremely convincing tone of Primary Art, that is, of Creation. To reject it leads either to sadness or to wrath.

It is not difficult to imagine the peculiar excitement and joy that one would feel, if any specially beautiful fairy-story were found to be "primarily" true, its narrative to be history, without thereby necessarily losing the mythical or allegorical significance that it had possessed. It is not difficult, for one is not called upon to try and conceive anything of a quality unknown. The joy would have exactly the same quality, if not the same degree, as the joy which the "turn" in a fairy-story gives: such joy has the very taste of primary truth. (Otherwise its name would not be joy.) It looks forward (or backward: the direction in this regard is unimportant) to the Great Eucatastrophe. The Christian joy, the *Gloria*, is of the same kind; but it is pre-eminently (infinitely, if our capacity were not finite) high and joyous. But this story is supreme; and it is true. Art has been verified. God is the Lord, of angels, and of men — and of elves. Legend and History have met and fused.

But in God's kingdom the presence of the greatest does not depress the small. Redeemed Man is still man.

Story, fantasy, still go on, and should go on. The Evangelium has not abrogated legends; it has hallowed them, especially the "happy ending." The Christian has still to work, with mind as well as body, to suffer, hope, and die; but he may now perceive that all his bents and faculties have a purpose, which can be redeemed. So great is the bounty with which he has been treated that he may now, perhaps, fairly dare to guess that in Fantasy he may actually assist in the effoliation and multiple enrichment of creation. All tales may come true; and yet, at the last, redeemed, they may be as like and as unlike the forms that we give them as Man, finally redeemed, will be like and unlike the fallen that we know.

# ON FAIRY-STORIES
## NOTES

### A (page 14)

THE VERY ROOT (not only the use) of their "marvels" is satiric, a mockery of unreason; and the "dream" element is not a mere machinery of introduction and ending, but inherent in the action and transitions. These things children can perceive and appreciate, if left to themselves. But to many, as it was to me, *Alice* is presented as a fairy-story and while this misunderstanding lasts, the distaste for the dream-machinery is felt. There is no suggestion of dream in *The Wind in the Willows*. "The Mole had been working very hard all the morning, spring-cleaning his little house." So it begins, and that correct tone is maintained. It is all the more remarkable that A. A. Milne. so great an admirer of this excellent book, should have prefaced to his dramatized version a "whimsical" opening in which a child is seen telephoning with a daffodil. Or perhaps it is not very remarkable, for a perceptive admirer (as distinct from a great admirer) of the book would never have attempted to dramatize it. Naturally only the simpler ingredients, the pantomime, and the satiric beast-fable elements, are capable of presentation in this form. The play is, on the lower level of drama, tolerably good fun, especially for those who have not read the book; but some children that I took to see *Toad of Toad Hall*,

brought away as their chief memory nausea at the opening.
For the rest they preferred their recollections of the book.

### B (page 32)

OF COURSE, these details, as a rule, got into the tales, *even
in the days when they were real practices,* because they had
a story-making value. If I were to write a story in which it
happened that a man was hanged, that *might* show in later
ages, if the story survived — in itself a sign that the story
possessed some permanent, and more than local or temporary, value — that it was written at a period when men were
really hanged, as a legal practice. *Might:* the inference
would not, of course, in that future time be certain. For
certainty on that point the future inquirer would have to
know definitely when hanging was practised and when I
lived. I could have borrowed the incident from other times
and places, from other stories; I could simply have invented
it. But even if this inference happened to be correct, the
hanging-scene would only occur in the story, (*a*) because
I was aware of the dramatic, tragic, or macabre force of this
incident in my tale, and (*b*) because those who handed it
down felt this force enough to make them keep the incident
in. Distance of time, sheer antiquity and alienness, might
later sharpen the edge of the tragedy or the horror; but the
edge must be there even for the elvish hone of antiquity to
whet it. The least useful question, therefore, for literary
critics at any rate, to ask or to answer about Iphigeneia,
daughter of Agamemnon, is: Does the legend of her sacrifice at Aulis come down from a time when human-sacrifice
was commonly practised?

I say only "as a rule," because it is conceivable that what
is now regarded as a "story" was once something different in

intent: e.g. a record of fact or ritual. I mean "record" strictly. A story invented to explain a ritual (a process that is sometimes supposed to have frequently occurred) remains primarily a story. It takes form as such, and will survive (long after the ritual evidently) only because of its story-values. In some cases details that now are notable merely because they are strange may have once been so everyday and unregarded that they were slipped in casually: like mentioning that a man "raised his hat," or "caught a train." But such casual details will not long survive change in everyday habits. Not in a period of oral transmission. In a period of writing (and of rapid changes in habits) a story may remain unchanged long enough for even its casual details to acquire the value of quaintness or queerness. Much of Dickens now has this air. One can open today an edition of a novel of his that was bought and first read when things were so in everyday life as they are in the story, though these everyday details are now already as remote from our daily habits as the Elizabethan period. But that is a special modern situation. The anthropologists and folk-lorists do not imagine any conditions of that kind. But if they are dealing with unlettered oral transmission, then they should all the more reflect that in that case they are dealing with items whose primary object was story-building, and whose primary reason for survival was the same. The Frog-King (see p. 66) is not a *Credo,* nor a manual of totem-law: it is a queer tale with a plain moral.

## C (page 34)

As far as my knowledge goes, children who have an early bent for writing have no special inclination to attempt the writing of fairy-stories, unless that has been almost the sole

form of literature presented to them; and they fail most
markedly when they try. It is not an easy form. If children
have any special leaning it is to Beast-fable, which adults
often confuse with Fairy-story. The best stories by children
that I have seen have been either "realistic" (in intent), or
have had as their characters animals and birds, who were in
the main the zoomorphic human beings usual in Beast-fable.
I imagine that this form is so often adopted principally because it allows a large measure of realism: the representation of domestic events and talk that children really know.
The form itself is, however, as a rule, suggested or imposed
by adults. It has a curious preponderance in the literature,
good and bad, that is nowadays commonly presented to
young children: I suppose it is felt to go with "Natural History," semi-scientific books about beasts and birds that are
also considered to be proper pabulum for the young. And
it is reinforced by the bears and rabbits that seem in recent
times almost to have ousted human dolls from the play-
rooms even of little girls. Children make up sagas, often
long and elaborate, about their dolls. If these are shaped
like bears, bears will be the characters of the sagas; but they
will talk like people.

## D (page 41)

I WAS INTRODUCED to zoology and palaeontology ("for
children") quite as early as to Faërie. I saw pictures of living beasts and of true (so I was told) prehistoric animals.
I liked the "prehistoric" animals best: they had at least lived
long ago, and hypothesis (based on somewhat slender evidence) cannot avoid a gleam of fantasy. But I did not like

being told that these creatures were "dragons." I can still re-feel the irritation that I felt in childhood at assertions of instructive relatives (or their gift-books) such as these: "snowflakes are fairy jewels," or "are more beautiful than fairy jewels"; "the marvels of the ocean depths are more wonderful than fairyland." Children expect the differences they feel but cannot analyse to be explained by their elders, or at least recognized, not to be ignored or denied. I was keenly alive to the beauty of "Real things," but it seemed to me quibbling to confuse this with the wonder of "Other things." I was eager to study Nature, actually more eager than I was to read most fairy-stories; but I did not want to be quibbled into Science and cheated out of Faërie by people who seemed to assume that by some kind of original sin I should prefer fairy-tales, but according to some kind of new religion I ought to be induced to like science. Nature is no doubt a life-study, or a study for eternity (for those so gifted); but there is a part of man which is not "Nature," and which therefore is not obliged to study it, and is, in fact, wholly unsatisfied by it.

## E (page 49)

THERE IS, for example, in surrealism commonly present a morbidity or un-ease very rarely found in literary fantasy. The mind that produced the depicted images may often be suspected to have been in fact already morbid; yet this is not a necessary explanation in all cases. A curious disturbance of the mind is often set up by the very act of drawing things of this kind, a state similar in quality and consciousness of morbidity to the sensations in a high fever, when the mind develops a distressing fecundity and facility in figure-making, seeing forms sinister or grotesque in all visible objects about it.

I am speaking here, of course, of the primary expression of Fantasy in "pictorial" arts, not of "illustrations"; nor of the cinematograph. However good in themselves, illustrations do little good to fairy-stories. The radical distinction between all art (including drama) that offers a *visible* presentation and true literature is that it imposes one visible form. Literature works from mind to mind and is thus more progenitive. It is at once more universal and more poignantly particular. If it speaks of *bread* or *wine* or *stone* or *tree*, it appeals to the whole of these things, to their ideas; yet each hearer will give to them a peculiar personal embodiment in his imagination. Should the story say "he ate bread," the dramatic producer or painter can only show "a piece of bread" according to his taste or fancy, but the hearer of the story will think of bread in general and picture it in some form of his own. If a story says "he climbed a hill and saw a river in the valley below," the illustrator may catch, or nearly catch, his own vision of such a scene; but every hearer of the words will have his own picture, and it will be made out of all the hills and rivers and dales he has ever seen, but specially out of The Hill, The River, The Valley which were for him the first embodiment of the word.

## F (page 51)

I AM REFERRING, of course, primarily to fantasy of forms and visible shapes. Drama can be made out of the impact upon human characters of some event of Fantasy, or Faërie, that requires no machinery, or that can be assumed or reported to have happened. But that is not fantasy in dramatic result; the human characters hold the stage and upon them attention is concentrated. Drama of this sort (exemplified by some of Barrie's plays) can be used frivolously, or it can be used for satire, or for conveying such "messages" as the playwright may have in his mind — for men. Drama is anthropocentric. Fairy-story and Fantasy need not be. There are, for instance, many stories telling how men and women have disappeared and spent years among the fairies, without noticing the passage of time, or appearing to grow older. In *Mary Rose* Barrie wrote a play on this theme. No fairy is seen. The cruelly tormented human beings are there all the time. In spite of the sentimental star and the angelic voices at the end (in the printed version) it is a painful play, and can easily be made diabolic: by substituting (as I have seen it done) the elvish call for "angel voices" at the end. The non-dramatic fairy-stories, in so far as they are concerned with the human victims, can also be pathetic or horrible. But they need not be. In most of them the fairies are also there, on equal terms. In some stories they are the real interest. Many of the short folk-lore accounts of such incidents purport to be just pieces of "evidence" about fairies, items in an agelong accumulation of "lore" concerning them and the modes of their existence. The sufferings of human beings who come into contact with them (often enough, wilfully) are thus seen in quite a different perspective. A drama could be made about the sufferings of a victim of research in radiology, but hardly about radium itself. But it is possible to be primarily interested in radium (not radiologists) — or primarily interested in Faërie, not tortured mortals. One interest will produce a scientific book, the other a fairy-story. Drama cannot well cope with either.

### G (page 66)

THE ABSENCE OF this sense is a mere hypothesis concerning men of the lost past, whatever wild confusions men of to-day, degraded or deluded, may suffer. It is just as legitimate an hypothesis, and one more in agreement with what little is recorded concerning the thoughts of men of old on this subject, that this sense was once stronger. That fantasies which blended the human form with animal and vegetable forms, or gave human faculties to beasts, are ancient is, of course, no evidence for confusion at all. It is, if anything, evidence to the contrary. Fantasy does not blur the sharp outlines of the real world; for it depends on them. As far as our western, European, world is concerned, this "sense of separation" has in fact been attacked and weakened in modern times not by fantasy but by scientific theory. Not by stories of centaurs or werewolves or enchanted bears, but by the hypotheses (or dogmatic guesses) of scientific writers who classed Man not only as "an animal" — that correct classification is ancient — but as "only an animal." There has been a consequent distortion of sentiment. The natural love of men not wholly corrupt for beasts, and the human desire to "get inside the skin" of living things, has run riot. We now get men who love animals more than men; who pity sheep so much that they curse shepherds as wolves; who weep over a slain war-horse and vilify dead soldiers. It is now, not in the days when fairy-stories were begotten, that we get "an absence of the sense of separation."

### H (page 68)

THE VERBAL ENDING — usually held to be as typical of the end of fairy-stories as "once upon a time" is of the beginning — "and they lived happily ever after" is an artificial device. It does not deceive anybody. End-phrases of this kind are to be compared to the margins and frames of pictures, and are no more to be thought of as the real end of any particular fragment of the seamless Web of Story than the frame is of the visionary scene, or the casement of the Outer World. These phrases may be plain or elaborate, simple or extravagant, as artificial and as necessary as frames plain, or carved, or gilded. "And if they have not gone away they are there still." "My story is done — see there is a little mouse; anyone who catches it may make himself a fine fur cap of it." "And they lived happily ever after." "And when the wedding was over, they sent me home with little paper shoes on a causeway of pieces of glass."

Endings of this sort suit fairy-stories, because such tales have a greater sense and grasp of the endlessness of the World of Story than most modern "realistic" stories, already hemmed within the narrow confines of their own small time. A sharp cut in the endless tapestry is not unfittingly marked by a formula, even a grotesque or comic one. It was an irresistible development of modern illustration (so largely photographic) that borders should be abandoned and the "picture" end only with the paper. This method may be suitable for photographs; but it is altogether inappropriate for the pictures that illustrate or are inspired by fairy-stories. An enchanted forest requires a margin, even an elaborate border. To print it conterminous with the page, like a "shot" of the Rockies in *Picture Post,* as if it were indeed a "snap" of fairyland or a "sketch by our artist on the spot," is a folly and an abuse.

As for the beginnings of fairy-stories: one can scarcely improve on the formula *Once upon a time.* It has an immediate effect. This effect can be appreciated by reading, for instance, the fairy-story *The Terrible Head* in the *Blue Fairy Book.* It is Andrew Lang's own adaptation of the story of Perseus and the Gorgon. It begins "once upon a time," and it does not name any year or land or person. Now this treatment does something which could be called "turning mythology into fairy-story." I should prefer to say that it turns high fairy-story (for such is the Greek tale) into a particular form that is at present familiar in our land: a nursery or "old wives" form. Namelessness is not a virtue but an accident, and should not have been imitated; for vagueness in this regard is a debasement, a corruption due to forgetfulness and lack of skill. But not so, I think, the timelessness. That beginning is not poverty-stricken but significant. It produces at a stroke the sense of a great uncharted world of time.

[Pages 85 and 86, illustrations in hard cover editions, have been deleted.]

# LEAF BY NIGGLE

THERE was once a little man called Niggle, who had a long journey to make. He did not want to go, indeed the whole idea was distasteful to him; but he could not get out of it. He knew he would have to start some time, but he did not hurry with his preparations.

Niggle was a painter. Not a very successful one, partly because he had many other things to do. Most of these things he thought were a nuisance; but he did them fairly well, when he could not get out of them: which (in his opinion) was far too often. The laws in his country were rather strict. There were other hindrances, too. For one thing, he was sometimes just idle, and did nothing at all. For another, he was kind-hearted, in a way. You know the sort of kind heart: it made him uncomfortable more often than it made him do anything; and even when he did anything, it did not prevent him from grumbling, losing his temper, and swearing (mostly to himself). All the same, it did land him in a good many odd jobs for his neighbour, Mr. Parish, a man with a lame leg. Occasionally he even helped other people from further off, if they came and asked him to. Also, now and again, he remembered his journey, and began to pack a few things in an ineffectual way: at such times he did not paint very much.

He had a number of pictures on hand; most of them were too large and ambitious for his skill. He was the sort of painter who can paint leaves better than trees. He used to spend a long time on a single leaf, trying to catch its shape, and its sheen, and the glistening of dewdrops on its edges. Yet he wanted to paint a whole tree, with all of its leaves in the same style, and all of them different.

There was one picture in particular which bothered him. It had begun with a leaf caught in the wind, and it became a tree; and the tree grew, sending out innumerable branches, and thrusting out the most fantastic roots. Strange birds came and settled on the twigs and had to be attended to. Then all round the Tree, and behind it, through the gaps in the leaves and boughs, a country began to open out; and there were glimpses of a forest marching over the land, and of mountains tipped with snow. Niggle lost interest in his other pictures; or else he took them and tacked them on to the edges of his great picture. Soon the canvas became so large that he had to get a ladder; and he ran up and down it, putting in a touch here, and rubbing out a patch there. When people came to call, he seemed polite enough, though he fiddled a little with the pencils on his desk. He listened to what they said, but underneath he was thinking all the time about his big canvas, in the tall shed that had been built for it out in his garden (on a plot where once he had grown potatoes).

He could not get rid of his kind heart. "I wish I was more strong-minded!" he sometimes said to himself, meaning that he wished other people's troubles did not make him feel uncomfortable. But for a long time he was not seriously perturbed. "At any rate, I shall get this one picture done, my real picture, before I have to go on that wretched journey," he used to say. Yet he was beginning to see that he could not put off his start indefinitely. The picture would have to stop just growing and get finished.

One day, Niggle stood a little way off from his picture and considered it with unusual attention and detachment. He could not make up his mind what he thought about it, and wished he had some friend who would tell him what to think. Actually it seemed to him wholly unsatisfactory, and yet very lovely, the only really beautiful picture in the world. What he would have liked at that moment would have been to see himself walk in, and slap him on the back, and say (with obvious sincerity): "Absolutely magnificent! I see exactly what you are getting at. Do get on with it, and don't bother about anything else! We will arrange for a public pension, so that you need not."

However, there was no public pension. And one thing he could see: it would need some concentration, some *work*, hard uninterrupted work, to finish the picture, even at its present size. He rolled up his sleeves, and began to concentrate. He tried for several days not to bother about other things. But there came a tremendous crop of interruptions. Things went wrong in his house; he had to go and serve on a jury in the town;

a distant friend fell ill; Mr. Parish was laid up with lumbago; and visitors kept on coming. It was springtime, and they wanted a free tea in the country: Niggle lived in a pleasant little house, miles away from the town. He cursed them in his heart, but he could not deny that he had invited them himself, away back in the winter, when he had not thought it an "interruption" to visit the shops and have tea with acquaintances in the town. He tried to harden his heart; but it was not a success. There were many things that he had not the face to say *no* to, whether he thought them duties or not; and there were some things he was compelled to do, whatever he thought. Some of his visitors hinted that his garden was rather neglected, and that he might get a visit from an Inspector. Very few of them knew about his picture, of course; but if they had known, it would not have made much difference. I doubt if they would have thought that it mattered much. I dare say it was not really a very good picture, though it may have had some good passages. The Tree, at any rate, was curious. Quite unique in its way. So was Niggle; though he was also a very ordinary and rather silly little man.

At length Niggle's time became really precious. His acquaintances in the distant town began to remember that the little man had got to make a troublesome journey, and some began to calculate how long at the latest he could put off starting. They wondered who would take his house, and if the garden would be better kept.

The autumn came, very wet and windy. The little painter was in his shed. He was up on the ladder, trying to catch the gleam of the westering sun on the peak

of a snow-mountain, which he had glimpsed just to the
left of the leafy tip of one of the Tree's branches. He
knew that he would have to be leaving soon: perhaps
early next year. He could only just get the picture finished, and only so so, at that: there were some corners
where he would not have time now to do more than hint
at what he wanted.

There was a knock on the door. "Come in!" he said
sharply, and climbed down the ladder. He stood on the
floor twiddling his brush. It was his neighbour, Parish:
his only real neighbour, all other folk lived a long way
off. Still, he did not like the man very much: partly because he was so often in trouble and in need of help;
and also because he did not care about painting, but
was very critical about gardening. When Parish looked
at Niggle's garden (which was often) he saw mostly
weeds; and when he looked at Niggle's pictures (which
was seldom) he saw only green and grey patches and
black lines, which seemed to him nonsensical. He did
not mind mentioning the weeds (a neighbourly duty),
but he refrained from giving any opinion of the pictures. He thought this was very kind, and he did not
realize that, even if it was kind, it was not kind enough.
Help with the weeds (and perhaps praise for the pictures) would have been better.

"Well, Parish, what is it?" said Niggle.

"I oughtn't to interrupt you, I know," said Parish
(without a glance at the picture). "You are very busy,
I'm sure."

Niggle had meant to say something like that himself,
but he had missed his chance. All he said was: "Yes."

"But I have no one else to turn to," said Parish.

"Quite so," said Niggle with a sigh: one of those sighs that are a private comment, but which are not made quite inaudible. "What can I do for you?"

"My wife has been ill for some days, and I am getting worried," said Parish. "And the wind has blown half the tiles off my roof, and water is pouring into the bedroom. I think I ought to get the doctor. And the builders, too, only they take so long to come. I was wondering if you had any wood and canvas you could spare, just to patch me up and see me through for a day or two." Now he did look at the picture.

"Dear, dear!" said Niggle. "You *are* unlucky. I hope it is no more than a cold that your wife has got. I'll come round presently, and help you move the patient downstairs."

"Thank you very much," said Parish, rather coolly. "But it is not a cold, it is a fever. I should not have bothered you for a cold. And my wife is in bed downstairs already. I can't get up and down with trays, not with my leg. But I see you are busy. Sorry to have troubled you. I had rather hoped you might have been able to spare the time to go for the doctor, seeing how I'm placed; and the builder too, if you really have no canvas you can spare."

"Of course," said Niggle; though other words were in his heart, which at the moment was merely soft without feeling at all kind. "I could go. I'll go, if you are really worried."

"I am worried, very worried. I wish I was not lame," said Parish.

So Niggle went. You see, it was awkward. Parish

was his neighbour, and everyone else a long way off. Niggle had a bicycle, and Parish had not, and could not ride one. Parish had a lame leg, a genuine lame leg which gave him a good deal of pain: that had to be remembered, as well as his sour expression and whining voice. Of course, Niggle had a picture and barely time to finish it. But it seemed that this was a thing that Parish had to reckon with and not Niggle. Parish, however, did not reckon with pictures; and Niggle could not alter that. "Curse it!" he said to himself, as he got out his bicycle.

It was wet and windy, and daylight was waning. "No more work for me today!" thought Niggle, and all the time that he was riding, he was either swearing to himself, or imagining the strokes of his brush on the mountain, and on the spray of leaves beside it, that he had first imagined in the spring. His fingers twitched on the handlebars. Now he was out of the shed, he saw exactly the way in which to treat that shining spray which framed the distant vision of the mountain. But he had a sinking feeling in his heart, a sort of fear that he would never now get a chance to try it out.

Niggle found the doctor, and he left a note at the builder's. The office was shut, and the builder had gone home to his fireside. Niggle got soaked to the skin, and caught a chill himself. The doctor did not set out as promptly as Niggle had done. He arrived next day, which was quite convenient for him, as by that time there were two patients to deal with, in neighbouring houses. Niggle was in bed, with a high temperature, and marvellous patterns of leaves and involved branches forming in his head and on the ceiling. It did

not comfort him to learn that Mrs. Parish had only had
a cold, and was getting up. He turned his face to the
wall and buried himself in leaves.

He remained in bed some time. The wind went on
blowing. It took away a good many more of Parish's
tiles, and some of Niggle's as well: his own roof began
to leak. The builder did not come. Niggle did not care;
not for a day or two. Then he crawled out to look for
some food (Niggle had no wife). Parish did not come
round: the rain had got into his leg and made it ache;
and his wife was busy mopping up water, and wondering if "that Mr. Niggle" had forgotten to call at the
builder's. Had she seen any chance of borrowing anything useful, she would have sent Parish round, leg or no
leg; but she did not, so Niggle was left to himself.

At the end of a week or so Niggle tottered out to his
shed again. He tried to climb the ladder, but it made
his head giddy. He sat and looked at the picture, but
there were no patterns of leaves or visions of mountains
in his mind that day. He could have painted a far-off
view of a sandy desert, but he had not the energy.

Next day he felt a good deal better. He climbed the
ladder, and began to paint. He had just begun to get
into it again, when there came a knock on the door.

"Damn!" said Niggle. But he might just as well have
said "Come in!" politely, for the door opened all the
same. This time a very tall man came in, a total stranger.

"This is a private studio," said Niggle. "I am busy.
Go away!"

"I am an Inspector of Houses," said the man, holding
up his appointment-card, so that Niggle on his ladder
could see it.

"Oh!" he said.

"Your neighbour's house is not satisfactory at all," said the Inspector.

"I know," said Niggle. "I took a note to the builders a long time ago, but they have never come. Then I have been ill."

"I see," said the Inspector. "But you are not ill now."

"But I'm not a builder. Parish ought to make a complaint to the Town Council, and get help from the Emergency Service."

"They are busy with worse damage than any up here," said the Inspector. "There has been a flood in the valley, and many families are homeless. You should have helped your neighbour to make temporary repairs and prevent the damage from getting more costly to mend than necessary. That is the law. There is plenty of material here: canvas, wood, waterproof paint."

"Where?" asked Niggle indignantly.

"There!" said the Inspector, pointing to the picture.

"My picture!" exclaimed Niggle.

"I dare say it is," said the Inspector. "But houses come first. That is the law."

"But I can't . . ." Niggle said no more, for at that moment another man came in. Very much like the Inspector he was, almost his double: tall, dressed all in black.

"Come along!" he said. "I am the Driver."

Niggle stumbled down from the ladder. His fever seemed to have come on again, and his head was swimming; he felt cold all over.

"Driver? Driver?" he chattered. "Driver of what?"

"You, and your carriage," said the man. "The carriage was ordered long ago. It has come at last. It's waiting. You start today on your journey, you know."

"There now!" said the Inspector. "You'll have to go; but it's a bad way to start on your journey, leaving your jobs undone. Still, we can at least make some use of this canvas now."

"Oh, dear!" said poor Niggle, beginning to weep. "And it's not, not even finished!"

"Not finished?" said the Driver. "Well, it's finished with, as far as you're concerned, at any rate. Come along!"

Niggle went, quite quietly. The Driver gave him no time to pack, saying that he ought to have done that before, and they would miss the train; so all Niggle could do was to grab a little bag in the hall. He found that it contained only a paint-box and a small book of his own sketches: neither food nor clothes. They caught the train all right. Niggle was feeling very tired and sleepy; he was hardly aware of what was going on when they bundled him into his compartment. He did not care much: he had forgotten where he was supposed to be going, or what he was going for. The train ran almost at once into a dark tunnel.

Niggle woke up in a very large, dim railway station. A Porter went along the platform shouting, but he was not shouting the name of the place; he was shouting *Niggle!*

Niggle got out in a hurry, and found that he had left his little bag behind. He turned back, but the train had gone away.

"Ah, there you are!" said the Porter. "This way!

What! No luggage? You will have to go to the Work-house."

Niggle felt very ill, and fainted on the platform. They put him in an ambulance and took him to the Workhouse Infirmary.

He did not like the treatment at all. The medicine they gave him was bitter. The officials and attendants were unfriendly, silent, and strict; and he never saw anyone else, except a very severe doctor, who visited him occasionally. It was more like being in a prison than in a hospital. He had to work hard, at stated hours: at digging, carpentry, and painting bare boards all one plain colour. He was never allowed outside, and the windows all looked inwards. They kept him in the dark for hours at a stretch, "to do some thinking," they said. He lost count of time. He did not even begin to feel better, not if that could be judged by whether he felt any pleasure in doing anything. He did not, not even in getting into bed.

At first, during the first century or so (I am merely giving his impressions), he used to worry aimlessly about the past. One thing he kept on repeating to himself, as he lay in the dark: "I wish I had called on Parish the first morning after the high winds began. I meant to. The first loose tiles would have been easy to fix. Then Mrs. Parish might never have caught cold. Then I should not have caught cold either. Then I should have had a week longer." But in time he forgot what it was that he had wanted a week longer for. If he worried at all after that, it was about his jobs in the hospital. He planned them out, thinking how quickly he could stop that board creaking, or rehang that door, or mend that table-leg. Probably he really became rather useful, though no one ever told him so. But that, of course, cannot have been the reason why they kept the poor little man so long. They may have been waiting for him to get better, and judging "better" by some odd medical standard of their own.

At any rate, poor Niggle got no pleasure out of life, not what he had been used to call pleasure. He was certainly not amused. But it could not be denied that he began to have a feeling of — well, satisfaction: bread rather than jam. He could take up a task the moment one bell rang, and lay it aside promptly the moment the next one went, all tidy and ready to be continued at the right time. He got through quite a lot in a day, now; he finished small things off neatly. He had no "time of his own" (except alone in his bed-cell), and yet he was becoming master of his time; he began to know just what he could do with it. There was no sense of rush. He was quieter inside now, and at resting-time he could really rest.

Then suddenly they changed all his hours; they hardly let him go to bed at all; they took him off carpentry altogether and kept him at plain digging, day after day. He took it fairly well. It was a long while before he even began to grope in the back of his mind for the curses that he had practically forgotten. He went on digging, till his back seemed broken, his hands were raw, and he felt that he could not manage another spadeful. Nobody thanked him. But the doctor came and looked at him.

"Knock off!" he said. "Complete rest — in the dark."

Niggle was lying in the dark, resting completely; so that, as he had not been either feeling or thinking at all, he might have been lying there for hours or for years, as far as he could tell. But now he heard Voices: not voices that he had ever heard before. There seemed to be a Medical Board, or perhaps a Court of Inquiry, going on close at hand, in an adjoining room with the door open, possibly, though he could not see any light.

"Now the Niggle case," said a Voice, a severe voice, more severe than the doctor's.

"What was the matter with him?" said a Second Voice, a voice that you might have called gentle, though it was not soft — it was a voice of authority, and sounded at once hopeful and sad. "What was the matter with Niggle? His heart was in the right place."

"Yes, but it did not function properly," said the First Voice. "And his head was not screwed on tight enough: he hardly ever thought at all. Look at the time he wasted, not even amusing himself! He never got ready for his journey. He was moderately well-off, and yet he arrived here almost destitute, and had to be put in the paupers' wing. A bad case, I am afraid. I think he should stay some time yet."

"It would not do him any harm, perhaps," said the Second Voice. "But, of course, he is only a little man. He was never meant to be anything very much; and he was never very strong. Let us look at the Records. Yes. There are some favourable points, you know."

"Perhaps," said the First Voice; "but very few that will really bear examination."

"Well," said the Second Voice, "there are these. He was a painter by nature. In a minor way, of course; still, a Leaf by Niggle has a charm of its own. He took a great deal of pains with leaves, just for their own sake. But he never thought that that made him important. There is no note in the Records of his pretending, even to himself, that it excused his neglect of things ordered by the law."

"Then he should not have neglected so many," said the First Voice.

"All the same, he did answer a good many Calls."

"A small percentage, mostly of the easier sort, and he called those Interruptions. The Records are full of the word, together with a lot of complaints and silly imprecations."

"True; but they looked like interruptions to him, of course, poor little man. And there is this: he never expected any Return, as so many of his sort call it. There is the Parish case, the one that came in later. He was Niggle's neighbour, never did a stroke for him, and seldom showed any gratitude at all. But there is no note in the Records that Niggle expected Parish's gratitude; he does not seem to have thought about it."

"Yes, that is a point," said the First Voice; "but rather small. I think you will find Niggle often merely forgot. Things he had to do for Parish he put out of his mind as a nuisance he had done with."

"Still, there is this last report," said the Second Voice, "that wet bicycle-ride. I rather lay stress on that. It seems plain that this was a genuine sacrifice: Niggle guessed that he was throwing away his last chance with his picture, and he guessed, too, that Parish was worrying unnecessarily."

"I think you put it too strongly," said the First Voice. "But you have the last word. It is your task, of course, to put the best interpretation on the facts. Sometimes they will bear it. What do you propose?"

"I think it is a case for a little gentle treatment now," said the Second Voice.

Niggle thought that he had never heard anything so generous as that Voice. It made Gentle Treatment sound like a load of rich gifts, and the summons to a King's feast. Then suddenly Niggle felt ashamed. To hear that he was considered a case for Gentle Treatment overwhelmed him, and made him blush in the dark. It was like being publicly praised, when you and all the audience knew that the praise was not deserved. Niggle hid his blushes in the rough blanket.

There was a silence. Then the First Voice spoke to Niggle, quite close. "You have been listening," it said.

"Yes," said Niggle.

"Well, what have you to say?"

"Could you tell me about Parish?" said Niggle. "I should like to see him again. I hope he is not very ill? Can you cure his leg? It used to give him a wretched time. And please don't worry about him and me. He was a very good neighbour, and let me have excellent potatoes very cheap, which saved me a lot of time."

"Did he?" said the First Voice. "I am glad to hear it."

There was another silence. Niggle heard the Voices

receding. "Well, I agree," he heard the First Voice say in the distance. "Let him go on to the next stage. To-morrow, if you like."

Niggle woke up to find that his blinds were drawn, and his little cell was full of sunshine. He got up, and found that some comfortable clothes had been put out for him, not hospital uniform. After breakfast the doctor treated his sore hands, putting some salve on them that healed them at once. He gave Niggle some good advice, and a bottle of tonic (in case he needed it). In the middle of the morning they gave Niggle a biscuit and a glass of wine; and then they gave him a ticket.

"You can go to the railway station now," said the doctor. "The Porter will look after you. Good-bye."

Niggle slipped out of the main door, and blinked a little. The sun was very bright. Also he had expected to walk out into a large town, to match the size of the station; but he did not. He was on the top of a hill, green, bare, swept by a keen invigorating wind. Nobody else was about. Away down under the hill he could see the roof of the station shining.

He walked downhill to the station briskly, but without hurry. The Porter spotted him at once.

"This way!" he said, and led Niggle to a bay, in which there was a very pleasant little local train standing: one coach, and a small engine, both very bright, clean, and newly painted. It looked as if this was their first run. Even the track that lay in front of the engine looked new: the rails shone, the chairs were painted green, and the sleepers gave off a delicious smell of fresh tar in the warm sunshine. The coach was empty.

"Where does this train go, Porter?" asked Niggle.

"I don't think they have fixed its name yet," said the Porter. "But you'll find it all right." He shut the door.

The train moved off at once. Niggle lay back in his seat. The little engine puffed along in a deep cutting with high green banks, roofed with blue sky. It did not seem very long before the engine gave a whistle, the brakes were put on, and the train stopped. There was no station, and no signboard, only a flight of steps up the green embankment. At the top of the steps there was a wicket-gate in a trim hedge. By the gate stood his bicycle; at least, it looked like his, and there was a yellow label tied to the bars with NIGGLE written on it in large black letters.

Niggle pushed open the gate, jumped on the bicycle, and went bowling downhill in the spring sunshine. Before long he found that the path on which he had started had disappeared, and the bicycle was rolling along over a marvellous turf. It was green and close; and yet he could see every blade distinctly. He seemed to remember having seen or dreamed of that sweep of grass somewhere or other. The curves of the land were familiar somehow. Yes: the ground was becoming level, as it should, and now, of course, it was beginning to rise again. A great green shadow came between him and the sun. Niggle looked up, and fell off his bicycle.

Before him stood the Tree, his Tree, finished. If you could say that of a Tree that was alive, its leaves opening, its branches growing and bending in the wind that

Niggle had so often felt or guessed, and had so often failed to catch. He gazed at the Tree, and slowly he lifted his arms and opened them wide.

"It's a gift!" he said. He was referring to his art, and also to the result; but he was using the word quite literally.

He went on looking at the Tree. All the leaves he had ever laboured at were there, as he had imagined them rather than as he had made them; and there were others that had only budded in his mind, and many that might have budded, if only he had had time. Nothing was written on them, they were just exquisite leaves, yet they were dated as clear as a calendar. Some of the most beautiful — and the most characteristic, the most perfect examples of the Niggle style — were seen to have been produced in collaboration with Mr. Parish: there was no other way of putting it.

The birds were building in the Tree. Astonishing birds: how they sang! They were mating, hatching, growing wings, and flying away singing into the Forest, even while he looked at them. For now he saw that the Forest was there too, opening out on either side, and marching away into the distance. The Mountains were glimmering far away.

After a time Niggle turned towards the Forest. Not because he was tired of the Tree, but he seemed to have got it all clear in his mind now, and was aware of it, and of its growth, even when he was not looking at it. As he walked away, he discovered an odd thing: the Forest, of course, was a distant Forest, yet he could approach it, even enter it, without its losing that particular charm.

He had never before been able to walk into the distance without turning it into mere surroundings. It really added a considerable attraction to walking in the country, because, as you walked, new distances opened out; so that you now had doubled, treble, and quadruple distances, doubly, trebly, and quadruply enchanting. You could go on and on, and have a whole country in a garden, or in a picture (if you preferred to call it that). You could go on and on, but not perhaps for ever. There were the Mountains in the background. They did get nearer, very slowly. They did not seem to belong to the picture, or only as a link to something else, a glimpse through the trees of something different, a further stage: another picture.

Niggle walked about, but he was not merely pottering. He was looking round carefully. The Tree was finished, though not finished with — "Just the other way about to what it used to be," he thought — but in the Forest there were a number of inconclusive regions, that still needed work and thought. Nothing needed altering any longer, nothing was wrong, as far as it had gone, but it needed continuing up to a definite point. Niggle saw the point precisely, in each case.

He sat down under a very beautiful distant tree — a variation of the Great Tree, but quite individual, or it would be with a little more attention — and he considered where to begin work, and where to end it, and how much time was required. He could not quite work out his scheme.

"Of course!" he said. "What I need is Parish. There are lots of things about earth, plants, and trees that he knows and I don't. This place cannot be left just as my private park. I need help and advice: I ought to have got it sooner."

He got up and walked to the place where he had decided to begin work. He took off his coat. Then, down in a little sheltered hollow hidden from a further view, he saw a man looking round rather bewildered. He was leaning on a spade, but plainly did not know what to do. Niggle hailed him. "Parish!" he called.

Parish shouldered his spade and came up to him. He still limped a little. They did not speak, just nodded as they used to do, passing in the lane; but now they walked about together, arm in arm. Without talking, Niggle and Parish agreed exactly where to make the small house and garden, which seemed to be required.

As they worked together, it became plain that Niggle was now the better of the two at ordering his time and getting things done. Oddly enough, it was Niggle who became most absorbed in building and gardening, while Parish often wandered about looking at trees, and especially at the Tree.

One day Niggle was busy planting a quickset hedge, and Parish was lying on the grass near by, looking attentively at a beautiful and shapely little yellow flower growing in the green turf. Niggle had put a lot of them among the roots of his Tree long ago. Suddenly Parish looked up: his face was glistening in the sun, and he was smiling.

"This is grand!" he said. "I oughtn't to be here, really. Thank you for putting in a word for me."

"Nonsense," said Niggle. "I don't remember what I said, but anyway it was not nearly enough."

"Oh yes, it was," said Parish. "It got me out a lot sooner. That Second Voice, you know: he had me sent here; he said you had asked to see me. I owe it to you."

"No. You owe it to the Second Voice," said Niggle. "We both do."

They went on living and working together: I do not know how long. It is no use denying that at first they occasionally disagreed, especially when they got tired. For at first they did sometimes get tired. They found that they had both been provided with tonics. Each bottle had the same label: *A few drops to be taken in water from the Spring, before resting.*

They found the Spring in the heart of the Forest; only once long ago had Niggle imagined it, but he had never drawn it. Now he perceived that it was the source of the lake that glimmered, far away and the nourishment of all that grew in the country. The few drops made the water astringent, rather bitter, but invigorating; and it cleared the head. After drinking they rested alone; and then they got up again and things went on merrily. At such times Niggle would think of wonderful new flowers and plants, and Parish always knew exactly how to set them and where they would do best. Long before the tonics were finished they had ceased to need them. Parish lost his limp.

As their work drew to an end they allowed themselves more and more time for walking about, looking at the trees, and the flowers, and the lights and shapes, and the lie of the land. Sometimes they sang together; but Niggle found that he was now beginning to turn his eyes, more and more often, towards the Mountains.

The time came when the house in the hollow, the garden, the grass, the forest, the lake, and all the country was nearly complete, in its own proper fashion. The Great Tree was in full blossom.

"We shall finish this evening," said Parish one day. "After that we will go for a really long walk."

They set out next day, and they walked until they came right through the distances to the Edge. It was not visible, of course: there was no line, or fence, or wall; but they knew that they had come to the margin of that country. They saw a man, he looked like a shepherd; he was walking towards them, down the grass-slopes that led up into the Mountains.

"Do you want a guide?" he asked. "Do you want to go on?"

For a moment a shadow fell between Niggle and Parish, for Niggle knew that he did now want to go on, and (in a sense) ought to go on; but Parish did not want to go on, and was not yet ready to go.

"I must wait for my wife," said Parish to Niggle. "She'd be lonely. I rather gathered that they would send her after me, some time or other, when she was ready, and when I had got things ready for her. The house is finished now, as well as we could make it; but I should like to show it to her. She'll be able to make it better, I expect: more homely. I hope she'll like this country, too." He turned to the shepherd. "Are you a guide?" he asked. "Could you tell me the name of this country?"

"Don't you know?" said the man. "It is Niggle's Country. It is Niggle's Picture, or most of it: a little of it is now Parish's Garden."

"Niggle's Picture!" said Parish in astonishment. "Did *you* think of all this, Niggle? I never knew you were so clever. Why didn't you tell me?"

"He tried to tell you long ago," said the man; "but you would not look. He had only got canvas and paint in those days, and you wanted to mend your roof with them. This is what you and your wife used to call Niggle's Nonsense, or That Daubing."

"But it did not look like this then, not *real*," said Parish.

"No, it was only a glimpse then," said the man; "but you might have caught the glimpse, if you had ever thought it worth while to try."

"I did not give you much chance," said Niggle. "I never tried to explain. I used to call you Old Earth-grubber. But what does it matter? We have lived and worked together now. Things might have been different, but they could not have been better. All the same, I am afraid I shall have to be going on. We shall meet again, I expect: there must be many more things we can do together. Good-bye!" He shook Parish's hand warmly: a good, firm, honest hand it seemed. He turned and looked back for a moment. The blossom on the Great Tree was shining like flame. All the birds were flying in the air and singing. Then he smiled, and nodded to Parish, and went off with the shepherd.

He was going to learn about sheep, and the high pasturages, and look at a wider sky, and walk ever further and further towards the Mountains, always uphill. Beyond that I cannot guess what became of him. Even little Niggle in his old home could glimpse the Moun-

tains far away, and they got into the borders of his picture; but what they are really like, and what lies beyond them, only those can say who have climbed them.

"I think he was a silly little man," said Councillor
Tompkins. "Worthless, in fact; no use to Society at all."

"Oh, I don't know," said Atkins, who was nobody of
importance, just a schoolmaster. "I am not so sure: it
depends on what you mean by *use*."

"No practical or economic use," said Tompkins. "I
dare say he could have been made into a serviceable cog
of some sort, if you schoolmasters knew your business.
But you don't, and so we get useless people of his sort.
If I ran this country I should put him and his like to
some job that they're fit for, washing dishes in a com-
munal kitchen or something, and I should see that
they did it properly. Or I would put them away. I
should have put *him* away long ago."

"Put him away? You mean you'd have made him start
on the journey before his time?"

"Yes, if you must use that meaningless old expression.
Push him through the tunnel into the great Rubbish
Heap: that's what I mean."

"Then you don't think painting is worth anything,
not worth preserving, or improving, or even making use
of?"

"Of course, painting has uses," said Tompkins. "But
you couldn't make use of his painting. There is plenty of
scope for bold young men not afraid of new ideas and
new methods. None for this old-fashioned stuff. Private day-dreaming. He could not have designed a

telling poster to save his life. Always fiddling with leaves and flowers. I asked him why, once. He said he thought they were pretty! Can you believe it? He said *pretty!* "What, digestive and genital organs of plants?" I said to him; and he had nothing to answer. Silly footler."

"Footler," sighed Atkins. "Yes, poor little man, he never finished anything. Ah well, his canvases have been put to 'better uses,' since he went. But I am not sure, Tompkins. You remember that large one, the one they used to patch the damaged house next door to his, after the gales and floods? I found a corner of it torn off, lying in a field. It was damaged, but legible: a mountain-peak and a spray of leaves. I can't get it out of my mind."

"Out of your what?" said Tompkins.

"Who are you two talking about?" said Perkins, intervening in the cause of peace: Atkins had flushed rather red.

"The name's not worth repeating," said Tompkins. "I don't know why we are talking about him at all. He did not live in town."

"No," said Atkins; "but you had your eye on his house, all the same. That is why you used to go and call, and sneer at him while drinking his tea. Well, you've got his house now, as well as the one in town, so you need not grudge him his name. We were talking about Niggle, if you want to know, Perkins."

"Oh, poor little Niggle!" said Perkins. "Never knew he painted."

That was probably the last time Niggle's name ever

came up in conversation. However, Atkins preserved the odd corner. Most of it crumbled; but one beautiful leaf remained intact. Atkins had it framed. Later he left it to the Town Museum, and for a long while "Leaf: by Niggle" hung there in a recess, and was noticed by a few eyes. But eventually the Museum was burnt down, and the leaf, and Niggle, were entirely forgotten in his old country.

"It is proving very useful indeed," said the Second Voice. "As a holiday, and a refreshment. It is splendid for convalescence; and not only for that, for many it is the best introduction to the Mountains. It works wonders in some cases. I am sending more and more there. They seldom have to come back."

"No, that is so," said the First Voice. "I think we shall have to give the region a name. What do you propose?"

"The Porter settled that some time ago," said the Second Voice. "*Train for Niggle's Parish in the bay:* he has shouted that for a long while now. Niggle's Parish. I sent a message to both of them to tell them."

"What did they say?"

"They both laughed. Laughed — the Mountains rang with it!"

# FARMER GILES
# OF HAM

Ægidii Ahenobarbi Julii Agricolæ de Hammo
Domini de Domito
Aulæ Draconariæ Comitis
Regni Minimi Regis et Basilei
m.ra facinora et mirabilis
exortus

or in the vulgar tongue

*The Rise and Wonderful Adventures of*
*Farmer Giles, Lord of Tame,*
*Count of Worminghall*
*and King of*
*the Little Kingdom*

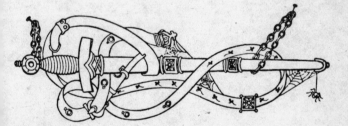

To C. H. Wilkinson

# FOREWORD

OF the history of the Little Kingdom few fragments have survived; but by chance an account of its origin has been preserved: a legend, perhaps, rather than an account; for it is evidently a late compilation, full of marvels, derived not from sober annals, but from the popular lays to which its author frequently refers. For him the events that he records lay already in a distant past; but he seems, nonetheless, to have lived himself in the lands of the Little Kingdom. Such geographical knowledge as he shows (it is not his strong point) is of that country, while of regions outside it, north or west, he is plainly ignorant.

An excuse for presenting a translation of this curious tale, out of its very insular Latin into the modern tongue of the United Kingdom, may be found in the glimpse that it affords of life in a dark period of the history of Britain, not to mention the light that it throws on the origin of some difficult place-names. Some may find the character and adventures of its hero attractive in themselves.

The boundaries of the Little Kingdom, either in time or space, are not easy to determine from the scanty evidence. Since Brutus came to Britain many kings and realms have come and gone. The partition under Locrin, Camber, and Albanac, was only the first of many shifting divisions. What with the love of petty independence on the one hand, and on the other the greed of kings for wider realms, the years were filled with swift alternations of war and peace, of mirth and woe, as historians of the reign of Arthur tell us: a time of unsettled frontiers, when men might rise or fall suddenly, and songwriters had abundant material and eager audiences. Somewhere in those long years, after the days of King Coel maybe, but before Arthur or the Seven Kingdoms of the English, we must place the events here related; and their scene is the valley of the Thames, with an excursion north-west to the walls of Wales.

The capital of the Little Kingdom was evidently, as is ours, in its south-east corner, but its confines are vague. It seems never to have reached far up the Thames into the West, nor beyond Otmoor to the North; its eastern borders are dubious. There are indications in a fragmentary legend of Georgius son of Giles and his page Suovetaurilius (Suet) that at one time an outpost against the Middle Kingdom was maintained at Farthingho. But that situation does not concern this story, which is now presented without alteration or further comment, though the original grandiose title has been suitably reduced to *Farmer Giles of Ham*.

# FARMER GILES OF HAM

ÆGIDIUS DE HAMMO was a man who lived in the midmost parts of the Island of Britain. In full his name was Ægidius Ahenobarbus Julius Agricola de Hammo; for people were richly endowed with names in those days, now long ago, when this island was still happily divided into many kingdoms. There was more time then, and folk were fewer, so that most men were distinguished. However, those days are now over, so I will in what follows give the man his name shortly, and in the vulgar form: he was Farmer Giles of Ham, and he had a red beard. Ham was only a village, but villages were proud and independent still in those days.

Farmer Giles had a dog. The dog's name was Garm. Dogs had to be content with short names in the vernacular: the Book-latin was reserved for their betters. Garm could not talk even dog-latin; but he could use the vulgar tongue (as could most dogs of his day) either to bully or to brag or to wheedle in. Bullying was for beggars and trespassers, bragging for other dogs, and wheedling for his master. Garm was both proud and afraid of Giles, who could bully and brag better than he could.

The time was not one of hurry or bustle. But bustle has very little to do with business. Men did their work without it; and they got through a deal both of work and of talk. There was plenty to talk about, for memorable events occurred very frequently. But at the moment when this tale begins nothing memorable had, in fact, happened in Ham for quite a long time. Which suited Farmer Giles down to the ground: he was a slow sort of fellow, rather set in his ways, and taken up with his own affairs. He had his hands full (he said) keeping the wolf from the door: that is, keeping himself as fat and comfortable as his father before him. The dog was busy helping him. Neither of them gave much thought to the Wide World outside their fields, the village, and the nearest market.

But the Wide World was there. The forest was not far off, and away west and north were the Wild Hills, and the dubious marches of the mountain-country. And among other things still at large there were giants: rude and uncultured folk, and troublesome at times. There was one giant in particular, larger and more stupid than his fellows. I find no mention of his name in the histories, but it does not matter. He was very large, his walking-stick was like a tree, and his tread was heavy. He brushed elms aside like tall grasses; and he was the ruin of roads and the desolation of gardens, for his great feet made holes in them as deep as wells; if he stumbled into a house, that was the end of it. And all this damage he did wherever he went, for his head was far above the roofs of houses and left his feet to look after themselves. He was

near-sighted and also rather deaf. Fortunately he lived far off in the Wild, and seldom visited the lands inhabited by men, at least not on purpose. He had a great tumbledown house  away up in the mountains; but he had very few friends, owing to his deafness and his stupidity, and the scarcity of giants. He used to go out walking in the Wild Hills and in the empty regions at the feet of the mountains, all by himself.

One fine summer's day this giant went out for a walk, and wandered aimlessly along, doing a great deal of damage in the woods. Suddenly he noticed that the sun was setting, and felt that his suppertime was drawing near; but he discovered that he was in a part of the country that he did not know at all and had lost his way. Making a wrong guess at the right direction he walked and he walked until it was dark night. Then he sat down and waited for the moon to rise. Then he walked and walked in the moonlight, striding out with a will, for he was anxious to get home. He had left his best copper pot on the fire, and feared that the bottom would be burned. But his back was to the mountains, and he was already in the lands inhabited by men. He was, indeed, now drawing near to the farm of Ægidius Ahenobarbus Julius Agricola and the village called (in the vulgar tongue) Ham.

It was a fine night. The cows were in the fields, and Farmer Giles's dog had got out and gone for a walk on his own account. He had a fancy for moonshine, and rabbits. He had no idea, of course, that a giant was also out for a walk. That would have given him a good reason for going out without leave, but a still better reason for staying quiet in the kitchen. At about two o'clock the giant arrived in Farmer Giles's fields, broke the hedges, trampled on the crops, and flattened the mowing-grass. In five minutes he had done more damage than the royal fox-hunt could have done in five days.

Garm heard a thump-thump coming along the river-bank, and he ran to the west side of the low hill on which the farmhouse

stood, just to see what was happening. Suddenly he saw the giant stride right across the river and tread upon Galathea, the farmer's favourite cow, squashing the poor beast as flat as the farmer could have squashed a blackbeetle.

That was more than enough for Garm. He gave a yelp of fright and bolted home. Quite forgetting that he was out without leave, he came and barked and yammered underneath his master's bedroom window. There was no answer for a long time. Farmer Giles was not easily wakened.

"Help! help! help!" cried Garm.

The window opened suddenly and a well-aimed bottle came flying out.

"Ow!" said the dog, jumping aside with practised skill. "Help! help! help!"

Out popped the farmer's head. "Drat you, dog! What be you a-doing?" said he.

"Nothing," said the dog.

"I'll give you nothing! I'll flay the skin off you in the morning," said the farmer, slamming the window.

"Help! help! help!" cried the dog.

Out came Giles's head again. "I'll kill you, if you make another sound," he said. "What's come to you, you fool?"

"Nothing," said the dog; "but something's come to you."

"What d'you mean?" said Giles, startled in the midst of his rage. Never before had Garm answered him saucily.

"There's a giant in your fields, an enormous giant;

and he's coming this way," said the dog. "Help! help! He is trampling on your sheep. He has stamped on poor Galathea, and she's as flat as a doormat. Help! help! He's bursting all your hedges, and he's crushing all your crops. You must be bold and quick, master, or you will soon have nothing left. Help!" Garm began to howl.

"Shut up!" said the farmer, and he shut the window. "Lord-a-mercy!" he said to himself; and though the night was warm, he shivered and shook.

"Get back to bed and don't be a fool!" said his wife. "And drown that dog in the morning. There is no call to believe what a dog says: they'll tell any tale, when caught truant or thieving."

"May be, Agatha," said he, "and may be not. But there's something going on in my fields, or Garm's a rabbit. That dog was frightened. And why should he come yammering in the night when he could sneak in at the back door with the milk in the morning?"

"Don't stand there arguing!" said she. "If you believe the dog, then take his advice: be bold and quick!"

"Easier said than done," answered Giles; for, indeed, he believed quite half of Garm's tale. In the small hours of the night giants seem less unlikely.

Still, property is property; and Farmer Giles had a short way with trespassers that few could outface. So he pulled on his breeches, and went down into the kitchen and took his blunderbuss from the wall. Some may well ask what a blunderbuss was. Indeed, this very question, it is said, was put to the Four Wise Clerks of Oxenford, and after thought they replied: "A blunderbuss is a short gun with a large bore firing many balls or  slugs, and capable of doing execution within a limited range without exact aim. (Now superseded in civilized countries by other firearms.)"

However, Farmer Giles's blunderbuss had a wide mouth that opened like a horn, and it did not fire balls or slugs, but anything that he could spare to stuff in. And it did not do execution, because he seldom loaded it, and never let it off. The sight of it was usually enough for his purpose. And this country was not yet civilized, for the blunderbuss was not superseded: it was indeed the only kind of gun that there was, and rare at that. People preferred bows and arrows and used gunpowder mostly for fireworks.

Well then, Farmer Giles took down the blunderbuss, and he put in a good charge of powder, just in case extreme measures should be required; and into the wide mouth he stuffed old nails and bits of wire, pieces of broken pot, bones and stones and other rubbish. Then he drew on his top-boots and his overcoat, and he went out through the kitchen garden.

The moon was low behind him, and he could see nothing worse than the long black shadows of bushes and trees; but he could hear a dreadful stamping-stumping coming up the side of the hill. He did not feel either bold or quick, whatever Agatha might say; but he was more anxious about his property than his skin. So, feeling a bit loose about the belt, he walked towards the brow of the hill.

Suddenly up over the edge of it the giant's face appeared, pale in the moonlight, which glittered in his large round eyes. His feet were still far below, making holes in the fields. The moon dazzled the giant and he did not see the farmer; but Farmer Giles saw him and was scared out of his wits. He pulled the trigger without thinking, and the blunderbuss went off with a staggering bang. By luck it was pointed more or less at the giant's large ugly face. Out flew the rubbish, and the stones and the bones, and the bits of crock and wire, and half a dozen nails. And since the range was indeed limited, by chance and no choice of the farmer's many of these things struck the giant: a piece of pot went in his eye, and a large nail stuck in his nose.

"Blast!" said the giant in his vulgar fashion. "I'm stung!" The noise had made no impression on him (he was rather deaf), but he did not like the nail. It was a long time since he had met any insect fierce enough to pierce his thick skin; but he had heard tell that away East, in the Fens, there were dragonflies that could bite like hot pincers. He thought that he must have run into something of the kind.

"Nasty unhealthy parts, evidently," said he. "I shan't go any further this way tonight."

So he picked up a couple of sheep off the hill-side, to eat when he got home, and went back over the river, making off about nor-nor-west at a great pace. He found his way home again in the end, for he was at last going in the right direction; but the bottom was burned off his copper pot.

As for Farmer Giles, when the blunderbuss went off it knocked him over flat on his back; and there he lay looking at the sky and wondering if the giant's feet would miss him as they passed by. But nothing happened, and the stamping-stumping died away in the distance. So he got up, rubbed his shoulder, and picked up the blunderbuss. Then suddenly he heard the sound of people cheering.

Most of the people of Ham had been looking out of their windows; a few had put on their clothes and come out (after the giant had gone away). Some were now running up the hill shouting.

The villagers had heard the horrible thump-thump of the giant's feet, and most of them had immediately got under the bed-clothes; some had got under the beds. But Garm was both proud and frightened of his master. He thought him terrible and splendid, when he was angry; and he naturally thought that any giant would think the same. So, as soon as he saw Giles come out with the blunderbuss (a sign of great wrath as a rule), he rushed off to the village, barking and crying:

"Come out! Come out! Come out! Get up! Get up! Come and see my great master! He is bold and quick. He is going to shoot a giant for trespassing. Come out!"

The top of the hill could be seen from most of the houses. When the people and the dog saw the giant's face rise above it, they quailed and held their breath, and all but the dog among them thought that this would prove a matter too big for Giles to deal with. Then the blunderbuss went bang, and the giant turned suddenly and went away, and in their amazement and their joy they clapped and cheered, and Garm nearly barked his head off.

"Hooray!" they shouted. "That will learn him! Master Ægidius has given him what for. Now he will go home and die, and serve him right and proper." Then they all cheered again together. But even as they cheered, they took note for their own profit that after all this blunderbuss could really be fired. There had been some debate in the village inns on that point; but now the matter was settled. Farmer Giles had little trouble with trespassers after that.

When all seemed safe some of the bolder folk came right up the hill and shook hands with Farmer Giles. A few—the parson, and the blacksmith, and the miller, and one or two other persons of importance—slapped him on the back. That did not please him (his shoulder was very sore), but he felt obliged to invite them into his house. They sat round in the

kitchen drinking his health and loudly praising him.
He made no effort to hide his yawns, but as long as
the drink lasted they took no notice. By the time they
had all had one or two (and the farmer two or three),
he began to feel quite bold; when they had all had
two or three (and he himself five or six), he felt as
bold as his dog thought him. They parted good
friends; and he slapped their backs heartily. His hands
were large, red, and thick; so he had his revenge.

Next day he found that the news had grown in the
telling, and he had become an important local figure.
By the middle of the next week the news had spread
to all the villages within twenty miles. He had
become the Hero of the Countryside. Very pleasant
he found it. Next market day he got enough free
drink to float a boat: that is to say, he nearly had his
fill, and came home singing old heroic songs.

At last even the King got to hear of it. The capital
of that realm, the Middle Kingdom of the island in

those happy days, was some twenty leagues distant from Ham, and they paid little heed at court, as a rule, to the doings of rustics in the provinces. But so

prompt an expulsion of a giant so injurious seemed worthy of note and of some little courtesy. So in due course—that is, in about three months, and on the feast of St. Michael—the King sent a magnificent letter. It was written in red upon white parchment, and expressed the royal approbation of "our loyal subject and well-beloved Ægidius Ahenobarbus Julius Agricola de Hammo."

The letter was signed with a red blot; but the court scribe had added: Ego Augustus Bonifacius Ambrosius Aurelianus Antoninus Pius et Magnificus, dux, rex, tyrannus, et Basileus Mediterranearum Partium, subscribo; and a large red seal was attached. So the document was plainly genuine. It afforded great pleasure to Giles, and was much admired, especially when it was discovered that one could get a seat and a drink by the farmer's fire by asking to look at it.

Better than the testimonial was the accompanying gift. The King sent a belt and a long sword. To tell

the truth the King had never used the sword himself. It belonged to the family and had been hanging in his armoury time out of mind. The armourer could not say how it came there, or what might be the use of it. Plain heavy swords of that kind were out of fashion at court just then, so the King thought it the very thing for a present to a rustic. But Farmer Giles was delighted, and his local reputation became enormous.

Giles much enjoyed the turn of events. So did his dog. He never got his promised whipping. Giles was a just man according to his lights; in his heart he gave a fair share of the credit to Garm, though he never went so far as to mention it. He continued to

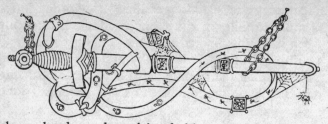

throw hard words and hard things at the dog when he felt inclined, but he winked at many little outings. Garm took to walking far afield. The farmer went about with a high step, and luck smiled on him. The autumn and early winter work went well. All seemed set fair—until the dragon came.

In those days dragons were already getting scarce in the island. None had been seen in the midland realm of Augustus Bonifacius for many a year. There were, of course, the dubious marches and the uninhabited mountains, westward and northward, but they were a long way off. In those parts once upon a time there had dwelt a number of dragons of one kind and another, and they had made raids far and wide. But the Middle Kingdom was in those days famous for the daring of the King's knights, and so many stray dragons had been killed, or had returned with grave damage. that the others gave up going that way.

It was still the custom for Dragon's Tail to be served up at the King's Christmas Feast; and each year a knight was chosen for the duty of hunting. He was supposed to set out upon St. Nicholas' Day and come home with a dragon's tail not later than the eve of the feast. But for many years now the Royal Cook had made a marvellous confection, a Mock Dragon's

Tail of cake and almond-paste, with cunning scales of hard icing-sugar. The chosen knight then carried this into the hall on Christmas Eve, while the fiddles played and the trumpets rang. The Mock Dragon's Tail was eaten after dinner on Christmas Day, and everybody said (to please the cook) that it tasted much better than Real Tail.

That was the situation when a real dragon turned up again. The giant was largely to blame. After his adventure he used to go about in the mountains visiting his scattered relations more than had been his custom, and much more than they liked. For he was always trying to borrow a large copper pot. But whether he got the loan of one or not, he would sit and talk in his long-winded lumbering fashion about the excellent country down away East, and all the wonders of the Wide World. He had got it into his head that he was a great and daring traveller.

"A nice land," he would say, "pretty flat, soft to the feet, and plenty to eat for the taking: cows, you know, and sheep all over the place, easy to spot, if you look carefully."

"But what about the people?" said they.

"I never saw any," said he. "There was not a knight to be seen or heard, my dear fellows. Nothing worse than a few stinging flies by the river."

"Why don't you go back and stay there?" said they.

"Oh well, there's no place like home, they say," said he. "But maybe I shall go back one day when I have a mind. And anyway I went there once, which is more than most folk can say. Now about that copper pot."

"And these rich lands," they would hurriedly ask, "these delectable regions full of undefended cattle, which way do they lie? And how far off?"

"Oh," he would answer, "away east or sou'east. But it's a long journey." And then he would give such an exaggerated account of the distance that he had walked, and the woods, hills, and plains that he had crossed, that none of the other less long-legged giants ever set out. Still, the talk got about.

Then the warm summer was followed by a hard winter. It was bitter cold in the mountains and food

was scarce. The talk got louder. Lowland sheep and kine from the deep pastures were much discussed. The dragons pricked up their ears. They were hungry, and these rumours were attractive.

"So knights are mythical!" said the younger and less experienced dragons. "We always thought so."

"At least they may be getting rare," thought the older and wiser worms; "far and few and no longer to be feared."

There was one dragon who was deeply moved. Chrysophylax Dives was his name, for he was of ancient and imperial lineage, and very rich. He was cunning, inquisitive, greedy, well-armoured, but not over bold. But at any rate he was not in the least afraid of flies or insects of any sort or size; and he was mortally hungry.

So one winter's day, about a week before Christmas, Chrysophylax spread his wings and took off. He landed quietly in the middle of the night plump in the heart of the midland realm of Augustus Bonifacius rex et basileus. He did a deal of damage in a short while, smashing and burning, and devouring sheep, cattle, and horses.

This was in a part of the land a long way from Ham, but Garm got the fright of his life. He had gone off on a long expedition, and taking advantage of his master's favour he had ventured to spend a night or two away from home. He was following an engaging scent along the eaves of a wood, when he turned a corner and came suddenly upon a new and alarming smell; he ran indeed slap into the tail of

Chrysophylax Dives, who had just landed. Never did a dog turn his own tail round and bolt home swifter than Garm. The dragon, hearing his yelp, turned and snorted; but Garm was already far out of range. He ran all the rest of the night, and arrived home about breakfast-time.

"Help! help! help!" he cried outside the back door.

Giles heard, and did not like the sound of it. It reminded him that unexpected things may happen, when all seems to be going well.

"Wife, let that dratted dog in," said he, "and take a stick to him!"

Garm came bundling into the kitchen with his eyes starting and his tongue hanging out. "Help!" he cried.

"Now what have you been a-doing this time?" said Giles, throwing a sausage at him.

"Nothing," panted Garm, too flustered to give heed to the sausage.

"Well, stop doing it, or I'll skin you," said the farmer.

"I've done no wrong. I didn't mean no harm," said the dog. "But I came on a dragon accidental-like, and it frightened me."

The farmer choked in his beer. "Dragon?" said he. "Drat you for a good-for-nothing nosey-parker! What d'you want to go and find a dragon for, at this time of the year, and me with my hands full? Where was it?"

"Oh! North over the hills and far away, beyond the Standing Stones and all," said the dog.

"Oh, away there!" said Giles, mighty relieved. "They're queer folk in those parts, I've heard tell, and aught might happen in their land. Let them get on with it! Don't come worriting me with such tales. Get out!"

Garm got out, and spread the news all over the village. He did not forget to mention that his master was not scared in the least. "Quite cool he was, and went on with his breakfast."

People chatted about it pleasantly at their doors. "How like old times!" they said. "Just as Christmas is coming, too. So seasonable. How pleased the King will be! He will be able to have Real Tail this Christmas."

But more news came in next day. The dragon, it appeared, was exceptionally large and ferocious. He was doing terrible damage.

"What about the King's knights?" people began to say.

Others had already asked the same question. Indeed, messengers were now reaching the King from the villages most afflicted by Chrysophylax, and they said to him as loudly and as often as they dared: "Lord, what of your knights?"

But the knights did nothing; their knowledge of the dragon was still quite unofficial. So the King brought the matter to their notice, fully and formally, asking for necessary action at their early convenience. He was greatly displeased when he found that their convenience would not be early at all, and was indeed daily postponed.

Yet the excuses of the knights were undoubtedly sound. First of all, the Royal Cook had already made the Dragon's Tail for that Christmas, being a man who believed in getting things done in good time. It would not do at all to offend him by bringing in a real tail at the last minute. He was a very valuable servant.

"Never mind the Tail! Cut his head off and put an end to him!" cried the messengers from the villages most nearly affected.

But Christmas had arrived, and most unfortunately a grand tournament had been arranged for St. John's Day: knights of many realms had been invited and were coming to compete for a valuable prize. It was obviously unreasonable to spoil the chances of the Midland Knights by sending their best men off on a dragon-hunt before the tournament was over.

After that came the New Year Holiday.

But each night the dragon had moved; and each move had brought him nearer to Ham. On the night of New Year's Day people could see a blaze in the distance. The dragon had settled in a wood about ten miles away, and it was burning merrily. He was a hot dragon when he felt in the mood.

After that people began to look at Farmer Giles and whisper behind his back. It made him very uncomfortable; but he pretended not to notice it. The next day the dragon came several miles nearer. Then Farmer Giles himself began to talk loudly of the scandal of the King's knights.

"I should like to know what they do to earn their keep," said he.

"So should we!" said everyone in Ham.

But the miller added: "Some men still get knighthood by sheer merit, I am told. After all, our good Ægidius here is already a knight in a manner of speaking. Did not the King send him a red letter and a sword?"

"There's more to knighthood than a sword," said Giles. "There's dubbing and all that, or so I understand. Anyway I've my own business to attend to."

"Oh! but the King would do the dubbing, I don't doubt, if he were asked," said the miller. "Let us ask him, before it is too late!"

"Nay!" said Giles. "Dubbing is not for my sort.

I am a farmer and proud of it: a plain honest man, and honest men fare ill at court, they say. It is more in your line, Master Miller."

The parson smiled: not at the farmer's retort, for Giles and the miller were always giving one another as good as they got, being bosom enemies, as the saying was in Ham. The parson had suddenly been struck with a notion that pleased him, but he said no more at that time. The miller was not so pleased, and he scowled.

"Plain certainly, and honest perhaps," said he. "But do you have to go to court and be a knight before you kill a dragon? Courage is all that is needed, as only yesterday I heard Master Ægidius declare. Surely he has as much courage as any knight?"

All the folk standing by shouted: "Of course not!" and "Yes indeed! Three cheers for the Hero of Ham!"

Then Farmer Giles went home feeling very uncomfortable. He was finding that a local reputation may require keeping up, and that may prove awkward. He kicked the dog, and hid the sword in a cupboard in the kitchen. Up till then it had hung over the fireplace.

The next day the dragon moved to the neighbouring village of Quercetum (Oakley in the vulgar tongue). He ate not only sheep and cows and one or two persons of tender age, but he ate the parson too. Rather rashly the parson had sought to dissuade him from his evil ways. Then there was a terrible commotion. All the people of Ham came up the hill, headed by their own parson; and they waited on Farmer Giles.

"We look to you!" they said; and they remained standing round and looking, until the farmer's face was redder than his beard.

"When are you going to start?" they asked.

"Well, I can't start today, and that's a fact," said he. "I've a lot on hand with my cowman sick and all. I'll see about it."

They went away; but in the evening it was rumoured that the dragon had moved even nearer, so they all came back.

"We look to you, Master Ægidius," they said.

"Well," said he, "it's very awkward for me just now. My mare has gone lame, and the lambing has started. I'll see about it as soon as may be."

So they went away once more, not without some grumbling and whispering. The miller was sniggering. The parson stayed behind, and could not be got rid of. He invited himself to supper, and made some pointed remarks. He even asked what had become of the sword and insisted on seeing it.

It was lying in a cupboard on a shelf hardly long enough for it, and as soon as Farmer Giles brought it out in a flash it leaped from the sheath, which the farmer dropped as if it had been hot. The parson sprang to his feet, upsetting his beer. He picked the sword up carefully and tried to put it back in the sheath; but it would not go so much as a foot in, and it jumped clean out again, as soon as he took his hand off the hilt.

"Dear me! This is very peculiar!" said the parson, and he took a good look at both scabbard and blade. He was a lettered man, but the farmer could only spell out large uncials with difficulty, and was none too sure of the reading even of his own name. That is why he had never given any heed to the strange letters that could dimly be seen on sheath and sword. As for the King's armourer, he was so accustomed to runes, names, and other signs of power and significance upon swords and scabbards that he had not bothered his head about them; he thought them out of date, anyway.

But the parson looked long, and he frowned. He had expected to find some lettering on the sword or on the scabbard, and that was indeed the idea that had come to him the day before; but now he was surprised at what he saw, for letters and signs there were, to be sure, but he could not make head or tail of them.

"There is an inscription on this sheath, and some, ah, epigraphical signs are visible also upon the sword," he said.

"Indeed?" said Giles. "And what may that amount to?"

"The characters are archaic and the language barbaric," said the parson, to gain time. "A little closer inspection will be required." He begged the loan of the sword for the night, and the farmer let him have it with pleasure.

When the parson got home he took down many

learned books from his shelves, and he sat up far into the night. Next morning it was discovered that the dragon had moved nearer still. All the people of Ham barred their doors and shuttered their windows; and those that had cellars went down into them and sat shivering in the candle-light.

But the parson stole out and went from door to door; and he told, to all who would listen through a crack or a keyhole, what he had discovered in his study.

"Our good Ægidius," he said, "by the King's grace is now the owner of Caudimordax, the famous sword that in popular romances is more vulgarly called Tailbiter."

Those that heard this name usually opened the door. They all knew the renown of Tailbiter, for that sword had belonged to Bellomarius, the greatest of all the dragon-slayers of the realm. Some accounts made him the maternal great-great-grandfather of the King. The songs and tales of his deeds were many, and if forgotten at court, were still remembered in the villages.

"This sword," said the parson, "will not stay sheathed, if a dragon is within five miles; and without doubt in a brave man's hands no dragon can resist it."

Then people began to take heart again; and some unshuttered the windows and put their heads out. In the end the parson persuaded a few to come and join him; but only the miller was really willing. To see Giles in a real fix seemed to him worth the risk.

They went up the hill, not without anxious looks north across the river. There was no sign of the dragon. Probably he was asleep; he had been feeding very well all the Christmas-time.

The parson (and the miller) hammered on the farmer's door. There was no answer, so they hammered louder. At last Giles came out. His face was very red. He also had sat up far into the night, drinking a good deal of ale; and he had begun again as soon as he got up.

They all crowded round him, calling him Good Ægidius, Bold Ahenobarbus, Great Julius, Staunch Agricola, Pride of Ham, Hero of the Countryside. And they spoke of Caudimordax, Tailbiter, The Sword that would not be Sheathed, Death or Victory, The Glory of the Yeomanry, Backbone of the Country, and the Good of one's Fellow Men, until the farmer's head was hopelessly confused.

"Now then! One at a time!" he said, when he got a chance. "What's all this, what's all this? It's my busy morning, you know."

So they let the parson explain the situation. Then the miller had the pleasure of seeing the farmer in as tight a fix as he could wish. But things did not turn out quite as the miller expected. For one thing Giles had drunk a deal of strong ale. For another he had a queer feeling of pride and encouragement when he learned that his sword was actually Tailbiter. He had been very fond of tales about Bellomarius when he was a boy, and before he had learned sense he had sometimes wished that he could have a marvellous and heroic sword of his own. So it came over him all of a sudden that he would take Tailbiter and go dragon-hunting. But he had been used to bargaining all his life, and he made one more effort to postpone the event.

"What!" said he. "Me go dragon-hunting? In my old leggings and waistcoat? Dragon-fights need some kind of armour, from all I've heard tell. There isn't any armour in this house, and that's a fact," said he.

That was a bit awkward, they all allowed; but they sent for the blacksmith. The blacksmith shook his head. He was a slow, gloomy man, vulgarly known as Sunny Sam, though his proper name was Fabricius Cunctator. He never whistled at his work, unless some disaster (such as frost in May) had duly occurred after he had foretold it. Since he was daily foretelling disasters of every kind, few happened that he had not foretold, and he was able to take the credit of them. It was his chief pleasure; so naturally he was reluctant to do anything to avert them. He shook his head again.

"I can't make armour out of naught," he said. "And it's not in my line. You'd best get the carpenter to make you a wooden shield. Not that it will help you much. He's a hot dragon."

Their faces fell; but the miller was not so easily to be turned from his plan of sending Giles to the dragon, if he would go; or of blowing the bubble of his local reputation, if he refused in the end. "What about ring-mail?" he said. "That would be a help; and it need not be very fine. It would be for business and not for showing off at court. What about your old leather jerkin, friend Ægidius? And there is a great pile of links and rings in the smithy. I don't suppose Master Fabricius himself knows what may be lying there."

"You don't know what you are talking about," said the smith, growing cheerful. "If it's real ring-mail you mean, then you can't have it. It needs the skill of the dwarfs, with every little ring fitting into four others and all. Even if I had the craft, I should be working for weeks. And we shall all be in our graves before them," said he, "or leastways in the dragon."

They all wrung their hands in dismay, and the blacksmith began to smile. But they were now so alarmed that they were unwilling to give up the miller's plan and they turned to him for counsel.

"Well," said he, "I've heard tell that in the old days those that could not buy bright hauberks out of the Southlands would stitch steel rings on a leather shirt and be content with that. Let's see what can be done in that line!"

So Giles had to bring out his old jerkin, and the smith was hurried back to his smithy. There they rummaged in every corner and turned over the pile of old metal, as had not been done for many a year. At the bottom they found, all dull with rust, a whole heap of small rings, fallen from some forgotten coat, such as the miller had spoken of. Sam, more unwilling and gloomy as the task seemed more hopeful, was set to work on the spot, gathering and sorting and cleaning the rings; and when (as he was pleased to point out) these were clearly insufficient for one so broad of back and breast as Master Ægidius, they made him split up old chains and hammer the links into rings as fine as his skill could contrive.

They took the smaller rings of steel and stitched

them on to the breast of the jerkin, and the larger and clumsier rings they stitched on the back; and then, when still more rings were forthcoming, so hard was poor Sam driven, they took a pair of the farmer's breeches and stitched rings on to them. And up on a shelf in a dark nook of the smithy the miller found the old iron frame of a helmet, and he set the cobbler to work, covering it with leather as well as he could.

37

The work took them all the rest of that day, and all the next day—which was Twelfthnight and the eve of the Epiphany, but festivities were neglected. Farmer Giles celebrated the occasion with more ale than usual; but the dragon mercifully slept. For the moment he had forgotten all about hunger or swords.

Early on the Epiphany they went up the hill,  carrying the strange result of their handiwork. Giles was expecting them. He had now no excuses left to offer; so he put on the mail jerkin and the breeches. The miller sniggered. Then Giles put on his topboots and an old pair of spurs; and also the leather-covered helmet. But at the last moment he clapped an old felt hat over the helmet, and over the mail coat he threw his big grey cloak.

"What is the purpose of that, Master?" they asked.

"Well," said Giles, "if it is your notion to go dragon-hunting jingling and dingling like Canterbury Bells, it ain't mine. It don't seem sense to me to let a dragon know that you are coming along the road sooner than need be. And a helmet's a helmet, and a challenge to battle. Let the worm see only my old hat over the hedge, and maybe I'll get nearer before the trouble begins."

They had stitched on the rings so that they overlapped, each hanging loose over the one below, and jingle they certainly did. The cloak did something to stop the noise of them, but Giles cut a queer figure in his gear. They did not tell him so. They girded the belt round his waist with difficulty, and they hung the scabbard upon it; but he had to carry the sword, for it would no longer stay sheathed, unless held with main strength.

The farmer called for Garm. He was a just man according to his lights. "Dog," he said, "you are coming with me."

The dog howled. "Help! help!" he cried.

"Now stop it!" said Giles. "Or I'll give you worse than any dragon could. You know the smell of this worm, and maybe you'll prove useful for once."

Then Farmer Giles called for his grey mare. She gave him a queer look and sniffed at the spurs. But she let him get up; and then off they went, and none of them felt happy. They trotted through the village, and all the folk clapped and cheered, mostly from their windows. The farmer and his mare put as  good a face on it as they could; but Garm had no sense of shame and slunk along with his tail down.

They crossed the bridge over the river at the end of the village. When at last they were well out of sight, they slowed to a walk. Yet all too soon they passed out of the lands belonging to Farmer Giles and to other folk of Ham and came to parts that the dragon had visited. There were broken trees, burned hedges and blackened grass, and a nasty uncanny silence.

The sun was shining bright, and Farmer Giles began to wish that he dared shed a garment or two; and he wondered if he had not taken a pint too many. "A nice end to Christmas and all," he thought. "And I'll be lucky if it don't prove the end of me too." He mopped his face with a large handkerchief—green, not red; for red rags infuriate dragons, or so he had heard tell.

But he did not find the dragon. He rode down many lanes, wide and narrow, and over other farmers' deserted fields, and still he did not find the dragon. Garm was, of course, of no use at all. He kept just behind the mare and refused to use his nose.

They came at last to a winding road that had suffered little damage and seemed quiet and peaceful. After following it for half a mile Giles began to wonder whether he had not done his duty and all that his reputation required. He had made up his mind that he had looked long and far enough, and he was just thinking of turning back, and of his dinner, and of telling his friends that the dragon had seen him coming and simply flown away, when he turned a sharp corner.

There was the dragon, lying half across a broken hedge with his horrible head in the middle of the road. "Help!" said Garm and bolted. The grey mare sat down plump, and Farmer Giles went off backwards into a ditch. When he put his head out, there was the dragon wide awake looking at him.

"Good morning!" said the dragon. "You seem surprised."

"Good morning!" said Giles. "I am that."

"Excuse me," said the dragon. He had cocked a very suspicious ear when he caught the sound of rings jingling, as the farmer fell. "Excuse my asking, but were you looking for me, by any chance?"

"No, indeed!" said the farmer. "Who'd a' thought of seeing you here? I was just going for a ride."

He scrambled out of the ditch in a hurry and backed away towards the grey mare. She was now on her feet again and was nibbling some grass at the wayside, seeming quite unconcerned.

"Then we meet by good luck," said the dragon. "The pleasure is mine. Those are your holiday clothes, I suppose. A new fashion, perhaps?" Farmer Giles's felt hat had fallen off and his grey cloak had slipped open; but he brazened it out.

"Aye," said he, "brand-new. But I must be after that dog of mine. He's gone after rabbits, I fancy."

"I fancy not," said Chrysophylax, licking his lips (a sign of amusement). "He will get home a long time before you do, I expect. But pray proceed on your way, Master—let me see, I don't think I know your name?"

"Nor I yours," said Giles; "and we'll leave it at that."

"As you like," said Chrysophylax, licking his lips again, but pretending to close his eyes. He had a wicked heart (as dragons all have), but not a very bold one (as is not unusual). He preferred a meal that he did not have to fight for; but appetite had returned after a good long sleep. The parson of

41

Oakley had been stringy, and it was years since he had tasted a large fat man. He had now made up his mind to try this easy meat, and he was only waiting until the old fool was off his guard.

But the old fool was not as foolish as he looked, and he kept his eye on the dragon, even while he was trying to mount. The mare, however, had other ideas, and she kicked and shied when Giles tried to get up. The dragon became impatient and made ready to spring.

"Excuse me!" said he. "Haven't you dropped something?"

An ancient trick, but it succeeded; for Giles had indeed dropped something. When he fell he had dropped Caudimordax (or vulgarly Tailbiter), and there it lay by the wayside. He stooped to pick it up; and the dragon sprang. But not as quick as Tailbiter. As soon as it was in the farmer's hand, it leaped forward with a flash, straight at the dragon's eyes.

"Hey!" said the dragon, and stopped very short. "What have you got there?"

"Only Tailbiter, that was given to me by the King," said Giles.

"My mistake!" said the dragon. "I beg your pardon." He lay and grovelled, and Farmer Giles began to feel more comfortable. "I don't think you have treated me fair."

"How not?" said Giles. "And anyway why should I?"

"You have concealed your honourable name and pretended that our meeting was by chance; yet you are plainly a knight of high lineage. It used, sir, to be the custom of knights to issue a challenge in such cases, after a proper exchange of titles and credentials"

"Maybe it used, and maybe it still is," said Giles, beginning to feel pleased with himself. A man who has a large and imperial dragon grovelling before him may be excused, if he feels somewhat uplifted. "But you are making more mistakes than one, old worm. I am no knight. I am Farmer Ægidius of Ham, I am; and I can't abide trespassers. I've shot giants with my blunderbuss before now, for doing less damage than you have. And I issued no challenge neither."

The dragon was disturbed. "Curse that giant for a liar!" he thought. "I have been sadly misled. And now what on earth does one do with a bold farmer and a sword so bright and aggressive?" He could recall no precedent for such a situation. "Chrysophylax is my name," said he, "Chrysophylax the Rich. What can I do for your honour?" he added ingratiatingly, with one eye on the sword, and hoping to escape battle.

"You can take yourself off, you horny old var-

43

mint," said Giles, also hoping to escape battle. "I only want to be shut of you. Go right away from here, and get back to your own dirty den!" He stepped towards Chrysophylax, waving his arms as if he was scaring crows.

That was quite enough for Tailbiter. It circled flashing in the air; then down it came, smiting the dragon on the joint of the right wing, a ringing blow that shocked him exceedingly. Of course Giles knew very little about the right methods of killing a dragon, or the sword might have landed in a tenderer spot; but Tailbiter did the best it could in inexperienced hands. It was quite enough for Chrysophylax—he could not use his wing for days. Up he got and turned to fly, and found that he could not. The farmer sprang on the mare's back. The dragon began to run. So did the mare. The dragon galloped over a field puffing and blowing. So did the mare. The farmer bawled and shouted, as if he was watching a horse race; and all the while he waved Tailbiter. The faster the dragon ran the more bewildered he became; and all the while the grey mare put her best leg foremost and kept close behind him.

On they pounded down the lanes, and through the gaps in the fences, over many fields and across many brooks. The dragon was smoking and bellowing and

44

losing all sense of direction. At last they came suddenly to the bridge of Ham, thundered over it, and came roaring down the village street. There Garm had the impudence to sneak out of an alley and join in the chase.

All the people were at their windows or on the roofs. Some laughed and some cheered; and some beat tins and pans and kettles; and others blew horns and pipes and whistles; and the parson had the church bells rung. Such a to-do and an on-going had not been heard in Ham for a hundred years.

Just outside the church the dragon gave up. He lay down in the middle of the road and gasped. Garm came and sniffed at his tail, but Chrysophylax was past all shame.

"Good people, and gallant warrior," he panted, as Farmer Giles rode up, while the villagers gathered round (at a reasonable distance) with hayforks, poles, and pokers in their hands. "Good people, don't kill me! I am very rich. I will pay for all the damage I have done. I will pay for the funerals of all the people I have killed, especially the parson of Oakley; he shall have a noble cenotaph—though he was rather lean. I will give you each a really good present, if you will only let me go home and fetch it."

"How much?" said the farmer.

"Well," said the dragon, calculating quickly. He noticed that the crowd was rather large. "Thirteen and eightpence each?"

"Nonsense!" said Giles. "Rubbish!" said the people. "Rot!" said the dog.

"Two golden guineas each, and children half price?" said the dragon.

"What about dogs?" said Garm. "Go on!" said the farmer. "We're listening."

"Ten pounds and a purse of silver for every soul, and gold collars for the dogs?" said Chrysophylax anxiously.

"Kill him!" shouted the people, getting impatient.

"A bag of gold for everybody, and diamonds for the ladies?" said Chrysophylax hurriedly.

"Now you talking, but not good enough," said Farmer Giles. "You've left dogs out again," said

Garm. "What size of bags?" said the men. "How many diamonds?" said their wives.

"Dear me! dear me!" said the dragon. "I shall be ruined."

"You deserve it," said Giles. "You can choose between being ruined and being killed where you lie." He brandished Tailbiter, and the dragon cowered.

"Make up your mind!" the people cried, getting bolder and drawing nearer.

Chrysophylax blinked; but deep down inside him he laughed: a silent quiver which they did not observe. Their bargaining had begun to amuse him. Evidently they expected to get something out of it. They knew very little of the ways of the wide and wicked world —indeed, there was no one now living in all the realm who had had any actual experience in dealing with dragons and their tricks. Chrysophylax was getting his breath back, and his wits as well. He licked his lips.

"Name your own price!" he said.

Then they all began to talk at once. Chrysophylax listened with interest. Only one voice disturbed him: that of the blacksmith.

"No good 'll come of it, mark my words," said he. "A worm won't return, say what you like. But no good will come of it, either way."

"You can stand out of the bargain, if that's your mind," they said to him, and went on haggling, taking little further notice of the dragon.

Chrysophylax raised his head; but if he thought of springing on them, or of slipping off during the argument, he was disappointed. Farmer Giles was standing by, chewing a straw and considering; but Tailbiter was in his hand, and his eye was on the dragon.

"You lie where you be!" said he, "or you'll get what you deserve, gold or no gold."

The dragon lay flat. At last the parson was made spokesman and he stepped up beside Giles. "Vile Worm!" he said. "You must bring back to this spot all your ill-gotten wealth; and after recompensing

47

those whom you have injured we will share it fairly among ourselves. Then, if you make a solemn vow never to disturb our land again, nor to stir up any other monster to trouble us, we will let you depart with both your head and your tail to your own home. And now you shall take such strong oaths to return (with your ransom) as even the conscience of a worm must hold binding."

Chrysophylax accepted, after a plausible show of hesitation. He even shed hot tears, lamenting his ruin, till there were steaming puddles in the road; but no one was moved by them. He swore many oaths, solemn and astonishing, that he would return with all his wealth on the feast of St. Hilarius and St. Felix. That gave him eight days, and far too short a time for the journey, as even those ignorant of geography might well have reflected. Nonetheless, they let him go, and escorted him as far as the bridge.

"To our next meeting!" he said, as he passed over the river. "I am sure we shall all look forward to it."

"We shall indeed," they said. They were, of course, very foolish. For though the oaths he had taken should have burdened his conscience with sorrow and a great fear of disaster, he had, alas! no conscience at all. And if this regrettable lack in one of imperial lineage was beyond the comprehension of the simple, at the least the parson with his booklearning might have guessed it. Maybe he did. He was a grammarian, and could doubtless see further into the future than others.

The blacksmith shook his head as he went back to his smithy. "Ominous names," he said. "Hilarius and Felix! I don't like the sound of them."

48

The King, of course, quickly heard the news. It ran through the realm like fire and lost nothing in the telling. The King was deeply moved, for various reasons, not the least being financial; and he made up his mind to ride at once in person to Ham, where such strange things seemed to happen.

He arrived four days after the dragon's departure, coming over the bridge on his white horse, with many knights and trumpeters, and a large baggage-train. All the people had put on their best clothes and lined the street to welcome him. The cavalcade came to a halt in the open space before the church gate. Farmer Giles knelt before the King, when he was presented; but the King told him to rise, and actually patted him on the back. The knights pretended not to observe this familiarity.

The King ordered the whole village to assemble in Farmer Giles's large pasture beside the river; and

49

when they were all gathered together (including Garm, who felt that he was concerned), Augustus Bonifacius rex et basileus was graciously pleased to address them.

He explained carefully that the wealth of the miscreant Chrysophylax all belonged to himself as lord of the land. He passed rather lightly over his claim to be considered suzerain of the mountain-country (which was debatable); but "we make no doubt in any case," said he, "that all the treasure of this worm was stolen from our ancestors. Yet we are, as all know, both just and generous, and our good liege Ægidius shall be suitably rewarded; nor shall any of our loyal subjects in this place go without some token of our esteem, from the parson to the youngest child. For we are well pleased with Ham. Here at least a sturdy and uncorrupted folk still retain the ancient courage of our race." The knights were talking among themselves about the new fashion in hats.

The people bowed and curtsied, and thanked him humbly. But they wished now that they had closed with the dragon's offer of ten pounds all round, and kept the matter private. They knew enough, at any rate, to feel sure that the King's esteem would not rise to that. Garm noticed that there was no mention of dogs. Farmer Giles was the only one of them who was really content. He felt sure of some reward, and was mighty glad anyway to have come safely out of a nasty business with his local reputation higher than ever.

The King did not go away. He pitched his pavilions in Farmer Giles's field, and waited for January the fourteenth, making as merry as he could in a miserable village far from the capital. The royal retinue ate up nearly all the bread, butter, eggs, chickens, bacon and mutton, and drank up every drop of old ale there was in the place in the next three days. Then they began to grumble at short commons. But the King paid handsomely for everything (in tallies to be honoured later by the Exchequer, which he hoped would shortly be richly replenished); so the folk of Ham were well satisfied, not knowing the actual state of the Exchequer.

January the fourteenth came, the feast of Hilarius and of Felix, and everybody was up and about early. The knights put on their armour. The farmer put on his coat of home-made mail, and they smiled openly, until they caught the King's frown. The farmer also put on Tailbiter, and it went into its sheath as easy as butter, and stayed there. The parson looked hard at the sword, and nodded to himself. The blacksmith laughed.

Midday came. People were too anxious to eat much. The afternoon passed slowly. Still Tailbiter showed no sign of leaping from the scabbard. None of the watchers on the hill, nor any of the small boys who had climbed to the tops of tall trees, could see anything by air or by land that might herald the return of the dragon.

The blacksmith walked about whistling; but it was not until evening fell and the stars came out that the other folk of the village began to suspect that the dragon did not mean to come back at all. Still they recalled his many solemn and astonishing oaths and kept on hoping. When, however, midnight struck and the appointed day was over, their disappointment was deep. The blacksmith was delighted.

"I told you so," he said. But they were still not convinced.

"After all he was badly hurt," said some.

"We did not give him enough time," said others. "It is a powerful long way to the mountains, and he would have a lot to carry. Maybe he has had to get help."

But the next day passed and the next. Then they all gave up hope. The King was in a red rage. The victuals and drink had run out, and the knights were grumbling loudly. They wished to go back to the merriments of court. But the King wanted money.

He took leave of his loyal subjects, but he was short and sharp about it; and he cancelled half the tallies on the Exchequer. He was quite cold to Farmer Giles and dismissed him with a nod.

"You will hear from us later," he said, and rode off with his knights and his trumpeters.

The more hopeful and simple-minded thought that a message would soon come from the court to summon Master Ægidius to the King, to be knighted at the least. In a week the message came, but it was of different sort. It was written and signed in triplicate: one copy for Giles; one for the parson; and one to be nailed on the church door. Only the copy addressed to the parson was of any use, for the court-hand was peculiar and as dark to the folk of Ham as the Booklatin. But the parson rendered it into the vulgar tongue and read it from the pulpit. It was short and to the point (for a royal letter); the King was in a hurry.

"We Augustus B. A. A. P and M. rex et cetera make known that we have determined, for the safety of our realm and for the keeping of our honour, that the worm or dragon styling himself Chrysophylax the Rich shall be sought out and condignly punished for his misdemeanours, torts, felonies, and foul perjury. All the knights of our Royal Household are hereby commanded to arm and make ready to ride upon this quest, so soon as Master Ægidius A. J. Agricola shall arrive at this our court. Inasmuch as the said Ægidius has proved himself a trusty man and well able to deal with giants, dragons, and other enemies of the King's peace, now therefore we command him to ride forth at once, and to join the company of our knights with all speed."

People said this was a high honour and next-door to being dubbed. The miller was envious. "Friend Ægidius is rising in the world," said he. "I hope he will know us when he gets back."

"Maybe he never will," said the blacksmith.

"That's enough from you, old horse-face!" said the farmer, mighty put out. "Honour be blowed! If I get back even the miller's company will be welcome. Still, it is some comfort to think that I shall be missing you both for a bit." And with that he left them.

You cannot offer excuses to the King as you can to your neighbours; so lambs or no lambs, ploughing or none, milk or water, he had to get up on his grey mare and go. The parson saw him off.

"I hope you are taking some stout rope with you?" he said.

"What for?" said Giles. "To hang myself?"

"Nay! Take heart, Master Ægidius!" said the parson. "It seems to me that you have a luck that

54

you can trust. But take also a long rope, for you may need it, unless my foresight deceives me. And now farewell, and return safely!"

"Aye! And come back and find all my house and land in a pickle. Blast dragons!" said Giles. Then, stuffing a great coil of rope in a bag by his saddle, he climbed up and rode off.

He did not take the dog, who had kept well out of sight all the morning. But when he was gone, Garm slunk home and stayed there, and howled all the night, and was beaten for it, and went on howling.

"Help, ow help!" he cried. "I'll never see dear master again, and he was so terrible and splendid. I wish I had gone with him, I do."

"Shut up!" said the farmer's wife, "or you'll never live to see if he comes back or he don't."

The blacksmith heard the howls. "A bad omen," he said cheerfully.

Many days passed and no news came. "No news is bad news," he said, and burst into song.

When Farmer Giles got to court he was tired and dusty. But the knights, in polished mail and with shining helmets on their heads, were all standing by their horses. The King's summons and the inclusion of the farmer had annoyed them, and so they insisted on obeying orders literally, setting off the moment that Giles arrived. The poor farmer had barely time

55

to swallow a sop in a draught of wine before he was
off on the road again. The mare was offended. What
she thought of the King was luckily unexpressed, as
it was highly disloyal.

It was already late in the day. "Too late in the day
to start a dragon-hunt," thought Giles. But they did
not go far. The knights were in no hurry, once they

had started. They rode along at their leisure, in a
straggling line, knights, esquires, servants, and ponies
trussed with baggage; and Farmer Giles jogging
behind on his tired mare.

When evening came, they halted and pitched their
tents. No provision had been made for Farmer Giles
and he had to borrow what he could. The mare was
indignant, and she forswore her allegiance to the
house of Augustus Bonifacius.

The next day they rode on, and all the day after.
On the third day they descried in the distance the dim
and inhospitable mountains. Before long they were
in regions where the lordship of Augustus Bonifacius
was not universally acknowledged. They rode then
with more care and kept closer together.

On the fourth day they reached the Wild Hills and

the borders of the dubious lands where legendary creatures were reputed to dwell. Suddenly one of those riding ahead came upon ominous footprints in the sand by a stream. They called for the farmer.

"What are these, Master Ægidius?" they said.

"Dragon-marks," said he.

"Lead on!" said they.

So now they rode west with Farmer Giles at their head, and all the rings were jingling on his leather coat. That mattered little; for all the knights were laughing and talking, and a minstrel rode with them singing a lay. Every now and again they took up the refrain of the song and sang it all together, very loud and strong. It was encouraging, for the song was good—it had been made long before in days when battles were more common than tournaments; but it was unwise. Their coming was now known to all the creatures of that land, and the dragons were cocking their ears in all the caves of the West. There was no longer any chance of their catching old Chrysophylax napping.

As luck (or the grey mare herself) would have it, when at last they drew under the very shadow of the dark mountains, Farmer Giles's mare went lame. They had now begun to ride along steep and stony paths, climbing upwards with toil and ever-growing disquiet. Bit by bit she dropped back in the line, stumbling and limping and looking so patient and sad that at last Farmer Giles was obliged to get off and walk. Soon they found themselves right at the back among the pack-ponies; but no one took any notice of them. The knights were discussing points of precedence and etiquette, and their attention was distracted. Otherwise they would have observed that dragon-marks were now obvious and numerous.

They had come, indeed, to the places where Chrysophylax often roamed, or alighted after taking his daily exercise in the air. The lower hills, and the slopes on either side of the path, had a scorched and trampled look. There was little grass, and the twisted stumps of heather and gorse stood up black amid wide patches of ash and burned earth. The region had been a dragons' playground for many a year. A dark mountain-wall loomed up before them.

Farmer Giles was concerned about his mare; but he was glad of the excuse for no longer being so conspicuous. It had not pleased him to be riding at the head of such a cavalcade in these dreary and dubious places. A little later he was gladder still, and had reason to thank his fortune (and his mare). For just about midday—it being then the Feast of Candlemas, and the seventh day of their riding—Tailbiter leaped out of its sheath, and the dragon out of his cave.

Without warning or formality he swooped out to give battle. Down he came upon them with a rush and a roar. Far from his home he had not shown himself over bold, in spite of his ancient and imperial lineage. But now he was filled with a great wrath; for he was fighting at his own gate, as it were, and with all his treasure to defend. He came round a shoulder of the mountain like a ton of thunderbolts, with a noise like a gale and a gust of red lightning.

The argument concerning precedence stopped short. All the horses shied to one side or the other, and some of the knights fell off. The ponies and the baggage and the servants turned and ran at once. They had no doubt as to the order of precedence.

Suddenly there came a rush of smoke that smothered them all, and right in the midst of it the dragon crashed into the head of the line. Several of the knights were killed before they could even issue their formal challenge to battle, and several others were bowled over, horses and all. As for the remainder, their steeds took charge of them, and turned round and fled, carrying their masters off, whether they wished it or no. Most of them wished it indeed.

But the old grey mare did not budge. Maybe she was afraid of breaking her legs on the steep stony path. Maybe she felt too tired to run away. She knew in her bones that dragons on the wing are worse behind you than before you, and you need more speed than a race-horse for flight to be useful. Besides, she had seen this Chrysophylax before, and remembered chasing him over field and brook in her own country, till he lay down tame in the village high-street. Anyway she stuck her legs out wide, and she snorted. Farmer Giles went as pale as his face could manage, but he stayed by her side; for there seemed nothing else to do.

And so it was that the dragon, charging down the line, suddenly saw straight in front of him his old enemy with Tailbiter in his hand. It was the last thing he expected. He swerved aside like a great bat and collapsed on the hillside close to the road. Up came the grey mare, quite forgetting to walk lame.

Farmer Giles, much encouraged, had scrambled hastily on her back.

"Excuse me," said he, "but were you looking for me, by any chance?"

"No indeed!" said Chrysophylax. "Who would have thought of seeing you here? I was just flying about."

"Then we meet by good luck," said Giles, "and the pleasure is mine; for I was looking for *you*. What's more, I have a bone to pick with you, several bones in a manner of speaking."

The dragon snorted. Farmer Giles put up his arm to ward off the hot gust, and with a flash Tailbiter swept forward, dangerously near the dragon's nose.

"Hey!" said he, and stopped snorting. He began to tremble and backed away, and all the fire in him was chilled. "You have not, I hope, come to kill me, good master?" he whined.

"Nay! nay!" said the farmer. "I said naught about killing." The grey mare sniffed.

"Then what, may I ask, are you doing with all these knights?" said Chrysophylax. "Knights always kill dragons, if we don't kill them first."

"I'm doing nothing with them at all. They're naught to me," said Giles. "And anyway, they are all dead now or gone. What about what you said last Epiphany?"

"What about it?" said the dragon anxiously.

"You're nigh on a month late," said Giles, "and payment is overdue. I've come to collect it. You should beg my pardon for all the bother I have been put to."

"I do indeed!" said he. "I wish you had not troubled to come."

"It'll be every bit of your treasure this time, and no market-tricks," said Giles, "or dead you'll be, and I shall hang your skin from our church steeple as a warning."

"It's cruel hard!" said the dragon.

"A bargain's a bargain," said Giles.

"Can't I keep just a ring or two, and a mite of gold, in consideration of cash payment?" said he.

"Not a brass button!" said Giles. And so they kept on for a while, chaffering and arguing like folk at a fair. Yet the end of it was as you might expect; for whatever else might be said, few had ever outlasted Farmer Giles at a bargaining.

The dragon had to walk all the way back to his cave, for Giles stuck to his side with Tailbiter held mighty close. There was a narrow path that wound up and round the mountain, and there was barely room for the two of them. The mare came just behind and she looked rather thoughtful.

It was five miles, if it was a step, and stiff going; and Giles trudged along, puffing and blowing, but never taking his eye off the worm. At last on the west side of the mountain they came to the mouth of the cave. It was large and black and forbidding, and its brazen doors swung on great pillars of iron. Plainly it had been a place of strength and pride in days long forgotten; for dragons do not build such works nor delve such mines, but dwell rather, when they may, in the tombs and treasuries of mighty men and giants of old. The doors of this deep house were set wide, and in their shadow they halted. So far Chrysophylax had had no chance to escape, but coming now to his own gate he sprang forward and prepared to plunge in.

Farmer Giles hit him with the flat of the sword. "Woa!" said he. "Before you go in, I've something to say to you. If you ain't outside again in quick time with something worth bringing, I shall come in after you and cut off your tail to begin with."

The mare sniffed. She could not imagine Farmer Giles going down alone into a dragon's den for any money on earth. But Chrysophylax was quite prepared to believe it, with Tailbiter looking so bright and sharp and all. And maybe he was right, and the mare, for all her wisdom, had not yet understood the change in her master. Farmer Giles was backing his luck, and after two encounters was beginning to fancy that no dragon could stand up to him.

Anyway, out came Chrysophylax again in mighty quick time, with twenty pounds (troy) of gold and silver, and a chest of rings and necklaces and other pretty stuff.

"There!" said he.

"Where?" said Giles. "That's not half enough, if

that's what you mean. Nor half what you've got, I'll be bound."

"Of course not!" said the dragon, rather perturbed to find that the farmer's wits seemed to have become brighter since that day in the village. "Of course not! But I can't bring it all out at once."

"Nor at twice, I'll wager," said Giles. "In you go again, and out again double quick, or I'll give you a taste of Tailbiter!"

"No!" said the dragon, and in he popped and out again double quick. "There!" said he, putting down an enormous load of gold and two chests of diamonds.

"Now try again!" said the farmer, "And try harder!"

"It's hard, cruel hard," said the dragon, as he went back in again.

But by this time the grey mare was getting a bit anxious on her own account. "Who's going to carry all this heavy stuff home, I wonder?" thought she; and she gave such a long sad look at all the bags and the boxes that the farmer guessed her mind.

"Never you worry, lass!" said he. "We'll make the old worm do the carting."

"Mercy on us!" said the dragon, who overheard these words as he came out of the cave for the third time with the biggest load of all, and a mort of rich jewels like green and red fire. "Mercy on us! If I carry all this, it will be near the death of me, and a bag more I never could manage, not if you killed me for it."

"Then there is more still, is there?" said the farmer.

"Yes," said the dragon, "enough to keep me respectable." He spoke near the truth for a rare wonder, and wisely as it turned out. "If you will leave me what remains," said he very wily, "I'll be your friend for ever. And I will carry all this treasure back to your honour's own house and not to the King's. And I will help you to keep it, what is more," said he.

Then the farmer took out a toothpick with his left hand, and he thought very hard for a minute. Then "Done with you!" he said, showing a laudable discretion. A knight would have stood out for the whole hoard and got a curse laid upon it. And as likely as not, if Giles had driven the worm to despair, he would have turned and fought in the end, Tailbiter or no Tailbiter. In which case Giles, if not slain himself, would have been obliged to slaughter his transport and leave the best part of his gains in the mountains.

Well, that was the end of it. The farmer stuffed his pockets with jewels, just in case anything went wrong; and he gave the grey mare a small load to carry. All the rest he bound on the back of Chrysophylax in boxes and bags, till he looked like a royal pantechnicon. There was no chance of his flying, for his load was too great, and Giles had tied down his wings.

"Mighty handy this rope has turned out in the end!" he thought, and he remembered the parson with gratitude.

So off now the dragon trotted, puffing and blowing, with the mare at his tail, and the farmer holding out Caudimordax very bright and threatening. He dared try no tricks.

In spite of their burdens the mare and the dragon made better speed going back than the cavalcade had made coming. For Farmer Giles was in a hurry—not the least reason being that he had little food in his bags. Also he had no trust in Chrysophylax after his breaking of oaths so solemn and binding, and he wondered much how to get through a night without death or great loss. But before that night fell he ran again into luck; for they overtook half a dozen of the servants and ponies that had departed in haste and were now wandering at a loss in the Wild Hills. They scattered in fear and amazement, but Giles shouted after them.

"Hey, lads!" said he. "Come back! I have a job for you, and good wages while this packet lasts."

So they entered his service, being glad of a guide, and thinking that their wages might indeed come more regular now than had been usual. Then they rode on, seven men, six ponies, one mare, and a dragon; and Giles began to feel like a lord and stuck out his chest. They halted as seldom as they could. At night Farmer Giles roped the dragon to four pickets,

65                                                    E

one to each leg, with three men to watch him in turn. But the grey mare kept half an eye open, in case the men should try any tricks on their own account.

After three days they were back over the borders of their own country; and their arrival caused such wonder and uproar as had seldom been seen between the two seas before. In the first village that they stopped at food and drink was showered on them free, and half the young lads wanted to join in the procession. Giles chose out a dozen likely young fellows. He promised them good wages, and bought them such mounts as he could get. He was beginning to have ideas.

After resting a day he rode on again, with his new escort at his heels. They sang songs in his honour: rough and ready, but they sounded good in his ears. Some folk cheered and others laughed. It was a sight both merry and wonderful.

Soon Farmer Giles took a bend southward, and steered towards his own home, and never went near the court of the King nor sent any message. But the news of the return of Master Ægidius spread like fire from the West; and there was great astonishment and confusion. For he came hard on the heels of a royal proclamation bidding all the towns and villages to go into mourning for the fall of the brave knights in the pass of the mountains.

Wherever Giles went the mourning was cast aside, and bells were set ringing, and people thronged by the wayside shouting and waving their caps and their scarves. But they booed the poor dragon, till he began bitterly to regret the bargain he had made. It was most humiliating for one of ancient and

imperial lineage. When they got back to Ham all the
dogs barked at him scornfully. All except Garm: he
had eyes, ears, and nose only for his master. Indeed,
he went quite off his head, and turned somer-
saults all along the street.

Ham, of course, gave the farmer a
wonderful welcome; but probably
nothing pleased him more than
finding the miller at a loss for
a sneer and the blacksmith
quite out of countenance.

"This is not the end of the affair, mark
my words!" said he; but he could not
think of anything worse to say and hung his head
gloomily. Farmer Giles, with his six men and his
dozen likely lads and the dragon and all, went on up
the hill, and there they stayed quiet for a while. Only
the parson was invited to the house.

The news soon reached the capital, and forgetting
the official mourning, and their business as well,
people gathered in the streets. There was much
shouting and noise.

The King was in his great house, biting his nails
and tugging his beard. Between grief and rage (and
financial anxiety) his mood was so grim that no one
dared speak to him. But at last the noise of the town
came to his ears: it did not sound like mourning or
weeping.

"What is all the noise about?" he demanded. "Tell
the people to go indoors and mourn decently! It
sounds more like a goose-fair."

"The dragon has come back, lord," they answered.

67

"What!" said the King. "Summon our knights, or what is left of them!"

"There is no need, lord," they answered. "With Master Ægidius behind him the dragon is tame as tame. Or so we are informed. The news has not long come in, and reports are conflicting."

"Bless our Soul!" said the King, looking greatly relieved. "And to think that we ordered a Dirge to be sung for the fellow the day after tomorrow! Cancel it! Is there any sign of our treasure?"

"Reports say that there is a veritable mountain of it, lord," they answered.

"When will it arrive?" said the King eagerly. "A good man this Ægidius—send him in to us as soon as he comes!"

There was some hesitation in replying to this. At

last someone took courage and said: "Your pardon, lord, but we hear that the farmer has turned aside towards his own home. But doubtless he will hasten here in suitable raiment at the earliest opportunity."

"Doubtless," said the King. "But confound his raiment! He had no business to go home without reporting. We are much displeased."

The earliest opportunity presented itself, and passed, and so did many later ones. In fact, Farmer Giles had been back for a good week or more, and still no word or news of him came to the court.

On the tenth day the King's rage exploded. "Send for the fellow!" he said; and they sent. It was a day's hard riding to Ham, each way.

"He will not come, lord!" said a trembling messenger two days later.

"Lightning of Heaven!" said the King. "Command him to come on Tuesday next, or he shall be cast into prison for life!"

"Your pardon, lord, but he still will not come," said a truly miserable messenger returning alone on the Tuesday.

"Ten Thousand Thunders!" said the King. "Take this fool to prison instead! Now send some men to fetch the churl in chains!" he bellowed to those that stood by.

"How many men?" they faltered. "There's a dragon, and . . . and Tailbiter, and——."

"And broomstales and fiddlesticks!" said the King. Then he ordered his white horse, and summoned his knights (or what was left of them) and a company of men-at-arms, and he rode off in fiery anger. All the people ran out of their houses in surprise.

But Farmer Giles had now become more than the Hero of the Countryside: he was the Darling of the Land; and folk did not cheer the knights and men-at-arms as they went by, though they still took off their hats to the King. As he drew nearer to Ham the looks grew more sullen; in some villages the people shut their doors and not a face could be seen.

Then the King changed from hot wrath to cold anger. He had a grim look as he rode up at last to the river beyond which lay Ham and the house of the farmer. He had a mind to burn the place down. But there was Farmer Giles on the bridge, sitting on the grey mare with Tailbiter in his hand. No one else was to be seen, except Garm, who was lying in the road.

"Good morning, lord!" said Giles, as cheerful as day, not waiting to be spoken to.

The King eyed him coldly. "Your manners are unfit for our presence," said he; "but that does not excuse you from coming when sent for."

"I had not thought of it, lord, and that's a fact," said Giles. "I had matters of my own to mind, and had wasted time enough on your errands."

"Ten Thousand Thunders!" cried the King in a hot rage again. "To the devil with you and your insolence! No reward will you get after this; and you will be lucky if you escape hanging. And hanged you shall be, unless you beg our pardon here and now, and give us back our sword."

"Eh?" said Giles. "I have got my reward, I reckon. Finding's keeping, and keeping's having, we say

70

here. And I reckon Tailbiter is better with me than with your folk. But what are all these knights and men for, by any chance?" he asked. "If you've come on a visit, you'd be welcome with fewer. If you want to take me away, you'll need a lot more."

The King choked, and the knights went very red and looked down their noses. Some of the men-at-arms grinned, since the King's back was turned to them.

"Give me my sword!" shouted the King, finding his voice, but forgetting his plural.

"Give us your crown!" said Giles: a staggering remark, such as had never before been heard in all the days of the Middle Kingdom.

"Lightning of Heaven! Seize him and bind him!"

cried the King, justly enraged beyond bearing. "What do you hang back for? Seize him or slay him!"

The men-at-arms strode forward.

"Help! help! help!" cried Garm.

Just at that moment the dragon got up from under the bridge. He had lain there concealed under the far bank, deep in the river. Now he let off a terrible steam, for he had drunk many gallons of water. At once there was a thick fog, and only the red eyes of the dragon to be seen in it.

"Go home, you fools!" he bellowed. "Or I will tear you to pieces. There are knights lying cold in the mountain-pass, and soon there will be more in the river. All the King's horses and all the King's men!" he roared.

Then he sprang forward and struck a claw into the King's white horse; and it galloped away like the ten thousand thunders that the King mentioned so often. The other horses followed as swiftly: some had met this dragon before and did not like the memory. The men-at-arms legged it as best they could in every direction save that of Ham.

The white horse was only scratched, and he was not allowed to go far. After a while the King brought him back. He was master of his own horse at any rate; and no one could say that he was afraid of any man or dragon on the face of the earth. The fog was gone when he got back, but so were all his knights and his men. Now things looked very different with the King all alone to talk to a stout farmer with Tailbiter and a dragon as well.

But talk did no good. Farmer Giles was obstinate.

He would not yield, and he would not fight, though the King challenged him to single combat there and then.

"Nay, lord!" said he, laughing. "Go home and get cool! I don't want to hurt you; but you had best be off, or I won't be answerable for the worm. Good day!"

And that was the end of the Battle of the Bridge of Ham. Never a penny of all the treasure did the King get, nor any word of apology from Farmer Giles, who was beginning to think mighty well of himself. What is more, from that day the power of the Middle Kingdom came to an end in that neighbourhood. For many a mile round about men took Giles for their lord. Never a man could the King with all his titles get to ride against the rebel Ægidius; for he had become the Darling of the Land, and the matter of song; and it was impossible to suppress all the lays that celebrated his deeds. The favourite one dealt with the meeting on the bridge in a hundred mock-heroic couplets.

Chrysophylax remained long in Ham, much to the profit of Giles; for the man who has a tame dragon is naturally respected. He was housed in the tithe-barn, with the leave of the parson, and there he was guarded by the twelve likely lads. In this way arose the first of the titles of Giles: Dominus de Domito Serpente, which is in the vulgar Lord of the Tame Worm, or shortly of Tame. As such he was widely honoured; but he still paid a nominal tribute to the King: six oxtails and a pint of bitter, delivered on St. Matthias' Day, that being the date of the meeting on the bridge. Before long, however, he advanced the Lord to Earl, and the belt of the Earl of Tame was indeed of great length.

After some years he became Prince Julius Ægidius and the tribute ceased. For Giles, being fabulously rich, had built himself a hall of great magnificence, and gathered great strength of men-at-arms. Very bright and gay they were, for their gear was the best that money could buy.

Each of the twelve likely lads became a captain. Garm had a gold collar, and while he lived roamed at his will, a proud and happy dog, insuffer-

able to his fellows; for he expected all other dogs to accord him the respect due to the terror and splendour of his master. The grey mare passed to her days' end in peace and gave no hint of her reflections.

In the end Giles became a king, of course, the King of the Little Kingdom. He was crowned in Ham in the name of Ægidius Draconarius; but he was more often known as Old Giles Worming. For the vulgar tongue came into fashion at his court, and none of his speeches were in the Book-latin. His wife made a queen of great size and majesty, and she kept a tight hand on the household accounts. There was no getting round Queen Agatha—at least it was a long walk.

Thus Giles became at length old and venerable and had a white beard down to his knees, and a very

75

respectable court (in which merit was often rewarded), and an entirely new order of knighthood. These were the Wormwardens, and a dragon was their ensign; the twelve likely lads were the senior members.

It must be admitted that Giles owed his rise in a large measure to luck, though he showed some wits in the use of it. Both the luck and the wits remained with him to the end of his days, to the great benefit of his friends and his neighbours. He rewarded the parson very handsomely; and even the blacksmith and the miller had their bit. For Giles could afford to be generous. But after he became king he issued a strong law against unpleasant prophecy, and made milling a royal monopoly. The blacksmith changed to the trade of an undertaker; but the miller became an obsequious servant of the crown. The parson became a bishop, and set up his see in the church of Ham, which was suitably enlarged.

Now those who live still in the lands of the Little Kingdom will observe in this history the true explanation of the names that some of its towns and villages bear in our time. For the learned in such matters inform us that Ham, being made the chief town of the new realm, by a natural confusion between the Lord of Ham and the Lord of Tame, became known by the latter name, which it retains to this day; for Thame with an *h* is a folly without warrant. Whereas in memory of the dragon, upon whom their fame and fortune were founded, the Draconarii built themselves a great house, four miles north-west of Tame, upon the spot where Giles and Chrysophylax first made acquaintance. That place became known throughout the kingdom as Aula Draconaria, or in the vulgar Worminghall, after the king's name and his standard.

The face of the land has changed since that time, and kingdoms have come and gone; woods have fallen, and rivers have shifted, and only the hills remain, and they are worn down by the rain and the wind. But still that name endures; though men now call it Wunnle (or so I am told); for villages have fallen from their pride. But in the days of which this tale speaks Worminghall it was, and a Royal Seat, and the dragon-standard flew above the trees; and all things went well there and merrily, while Tailbiter was above ground.

Chrysophylax begged often for his liberty; and he proved expensive to feed, since he continued to grow, as dragons will, like trees, as long as there is life in them. So it came to pass, after some years, when Giles felt himself securely established, that he let the poor worm go back home. They parted with many expressions of mutual esteem, and a pact of non-aggression upon either side. In his bad heart of hearts the dragon felt as kindly disposed towards Giles as a dragon can feel towards anyone. After all there was Tailbiter: his life might easily have been taken, and all his hoard too. As it was, he still had a mort of treasure at home in his cave (as indeed Giles suspected).

He flew back to the mountains, slowly and laboriously, for his wings were clumsy with long disuse, and his size and his armour were greatly increased. Arriving home, he at once routed out a young dragon who had had the temerity to take up residence in his cave while Chrysophylax was away. It is said that the noise of the battle was heard throughout Venedotia. When, with great satisfaction, he had devoured his defeated opponent, he felt better, and the scars of his humiliation were assuaged, and he slept for a long while. But at last, waking suddenly, he set off in search of that tallest and stupidest of the giants, who had started all the trouble one summer's night long before. He gave him a piece of his mind, and the poor fellow was very much crushed.

"A blunderbuss, was it?" said he, scratching his head. "I thought it was horseflies!"

### Finis

*or in the vulgar*

**THE END**

J. R. R. TOLKIEN

# THE ADVENTURES
# OF TOM BOMBADIL

*and other verses
from The Red Book*

WITH ILLUSTRATIONS BY
PAULINE BAYNES

# PREFACE

The Red Book contains a large number of verses. A few are included in the narrative of the *Downfall of the Lord of the Rings*, or in the attached stories and chronicles; many more are found on loose leaves, while some are written carelessly in margins and blank spaces. Of the last sort most are nonsense, now often unintelligible even when legible, or half-remembered fragments. From these marginalia are drawn Nos. 4, 11, 13; though a better example of their general character would be the scribble, on the page recording Bilbo's *When winter first begins to bite*:

> *The wind so whirled a weathercock*
> *He could not hold his tail up;*
> *The frost so nipped a throstlecock*
> *He could not snap a snail up.*
> *'My case is hard' the throstle cried,*
> *And 'All is vane' the cock replied;*
> *And so they set their wail up.*

The present selection is taken from the older pieces, mainly concerned with legends and jests of the Shire at the end of the Third Age, that appear to have been made by Hobbits, especially by Bilbo and his friends, or their immediate descendants. Their authorship is, however, seldom indicated. Those outside the narratives are in various hands, and were probably written down from oral tradition.

In the Red Book it is said that No. 5 was made by Bilbo, and No. 7 by Sam Gamgee. No. 8 is marked SG, and the ascription may be accepted. No. 12 is also marked SG, though at most Sam can only have touched up an older piece of the comic bestiary lore of which Hobbits appear to have been fond. In *The Lord of the Rings* Sam stated that No. 10 was traditional in the Shire.

No. 3 is an example of another kind which seems to have amused Hobbits: a rhyme or story which returns to its own beginning, and so may be recited until the hearers revolt. Several specimens are found in the Red Book, but the others are simple and crude. No. 3 is much the longest and most elaborate. It was evidently made by Bilbo. This is indicated by its obvious relationship to the long poem recited by Bilbo, as his own composition, in the house of Elrond. In origin a 'nonsense rhyme', it is in the Rivendell version found transformed and applied, somewhat incongruously, to the High-elvish and Númenorean legends of Eärendil. Probably because Bilbo invented its metrical devices and was proud of them. They do not appear in other pieces in the Red Book. The older form, here given, must belong to the early days after Bilbo's return from his journey. Though the influence of Elvish traditions is seen, they are not seriously treated, and the names used (*Derrilyn*, *Thellamie*, *Belmarie*, *Aerie*) are mere inventions in the Elvish style, and are not in fact Elvish at all.

The influence of the events at the end of the Third Age, and the widening of the horizons of the Shire by contact with Rivendell and Gondor, is to be seen in other pieces. No. 6, though here placed next to Bilbo's Man-in-the-Moon rhyme, and the last item, No. 16, must be derived ultimately from Gondor. They are evidently based on the traditions of Men, living in shorelands and familiar with rivers running into the Sea. No. 6 actually mentions *Belfalas* (the windy bay of Bel), and the Sea-ward Tower, *Tirith Aear*, of Dol Amroth. No. 16 mentions the Seven Rivers[1] that flowed into the Sea in the South Kingdom, and uses the Gondorian name, of High-elvish form, *Fíriel*, mortal woman.[2] In the Langstrand and Dol Amroth there were many traditions of the ancient Elvish dwellings, and of the haven at the mouth of the Morthond from which 'westward ships' had sailed as far back as the fall of Eregion in the Second Age. These two pieces, therefore, are only re-handlings of Southern matter, though this may have reached Bilbo by way of Rivendell. No. 14 also depends on the lore of Rivendell, Elvish and Númenorean, concerning the heroic days at the end of the First Age; it seems to contain echoes of the Númenorean tale of Túrin and Mim the Dwarf.

Nos. 1 and 2 evidently come from the Buckland. They show more knowledge of that country, and of the Dingle, the wooded

---

[1] *Lefnui, Morthond-Kiril-Ringló, Gilrain-Sernui*, and *Anduin*.

[2] The name was borne by a princess of Gondor, through whom Aragorn claimed descent from the Southern line. It was also the name of a daughter of Elanor, daughter of Sam, but her name, if connected with the rhyme, must be derived from it; it could not have arisen in Westmarch.

valley of the Withywindle,[1] than any Hobbits west of the Marish were likely to possess. They also show that the Bucklanders knew Bombadil,[2] though, no doubt, they had as little understanding of his powers as the Shire-folk had of Gandalf's: both were regarded as benevolent persons, mysterious maybe and unpredictable but nonetheless comic. No. 1 is the earlier piece, and is made up of various hobbit-versions of legends concerning Bombadil. No. 2 uses similar traditions, though Tom's raillery is here turned in jest upon his friends, who treat it with amusement (tinged with fear); but it was probably composed much later and after the visit of Frodo and his companions to the house of Bombadil.

The verses, of hobbit origin, here presented have generally two features in common. They are fond of strange words, and of rhyming and metrical tricks—in their simplicity Hobbits evidently regarded such things as virtues or graces, though they were, no doubt, mere imitations of Elvish practices. They are also, at least on the surface, lighthearted or frivolous, though sometimes one may uneasily suspect that more is meant than meets the ear. No. 15, certainly of hobbit origin, is an exception. It is the latest piece and belongs to the Fourth Age; but it is included here, because a hand has scrawled at its head *Frodos Dreme*. That is remarkable, and though the piece is most unlikely to have been written by Frodo himself, the title shows that it was associated with the dark and despairing dreams which visited him in March and October during his last three years. But there were certainly other traditions concerning Hobbits that were taken by the 'wandering-madness', and if they ever returned, were afterwards queer and uncommunicable. The thought of the Sea was ever-present in the background of hobbit imagination; but fear of it and distrust of all Elvish lore, was the prevailing mood in the Shire at the end of the Third Age, and that mood was certainly not entirely dispelled by the events and changes with which that Age ended.

[1] *Grindwall* was a small hythe on the north bank of the Withywindle; it was outside the Hay, and so was well watched and protected by a *grind* or fence extended into the water. *Breredon* (Briar Hill) was a little village on rising ground behind the hythe, in the narrow tongue between the end of the High Hay and the Brandywine. At the *Mithe*, the outflow of the Shirebourn, was a landing-stage, from which a lane ran to Deephallow and so on to the Causeway road that went through Rushey and Stock.

[2] Indeed they probably gave him this name (it is Bucklandish in form) to add to his many older ones.

# I
# THE ADVENTURES OF
# TOM BOMBADIL

Old Tom Bombadil was a merry fellow;
bright blue his jacket was and his boots were yellow,
green were his girdle and his breeches all of leather;
he wore in his tall hat a swan-wing feather.
He lived up under Hill, where the Withywindle
ran from a grassy well down into the dingle.

Old Tom in summertime walked about the meadows
gathering the buttercups, running after shadows,
tickling the bumblebees that buzzed among the flowers,
sitting by the waterside for hours upon hours.

There his beard dangled long down into the water:
up came Goldberry, the River-woman's daughter;
pulled Tom's hanging hair. In he went a-wallowing
under the water-lilies, bubbling and a-swallowing.

'Hey, Tom Bombadil! Whither are you going?'
said fair Goldberry. 'Bubbles you are blowing,
frightening the finny fish and the brown water-rat,
startling the dabchicks, and drowning your feather-hat!'

'You bring it back again, there's a pretty maiden!'
said Tom Bombadil. 'I do not care for wading.
Go down! Sleep again where the pools are shady
far below willow-roots, little water-lady!'

Back to her mother's house in the deepest hollow
swam young Goldberry. But Tom, he would not follow;
on knotted willow-roots he sat in sunny weather,
drying his yellow boots and his draggled feather.

Up woke Willow-man, began upon his singing,
sang Tom fast asleep under branches swinging;
in a crack caught him tight: snick! it closed together,
trapped Tom Bombadil, coat and hat and feather.

'Ha, Tom Bombadil! What be you a-thinking,
peeping inside my tree, watching me a-drinking
deep in my wooden house, tickling me with feather,
dripping wet down my face like a rainy weather?'

'You let me out again, Old Man Willow!
I am stiff lying here; they're no sort of pillow,
your hard crooked roots. Drink your river-water!
Go back to sleep again like the River-daughter!'

Willow-man let him loose when he heard him speaking;
locked fast his wooden house, muttering and creaking,
whispering inside the tree. Out from willow-dingle
Tom went walking on up the Withywindle.
Under the forest-eaves he sat a while a-listening:
on the boughs piping birds were chirruping and whistling.
Butterflies about his head went quivering and winking,
until grey clouds came up, as the sun was sinking.

Then Tom hurried on. Rain began to shiver,
round rings spattering in the running river;
a wind blew, shaken leaves chilly drops were dripping;
into a sheltering hole Old Tom went skipping.

Out came Badger-brock with his snowy forehead
and his dark blinking eyes. In the hill he quarried
with his wife and many sons. By the coat they caught him,
pulled him inside their earth, down their tunnels brought him.

Inside their secret house, there they sat a-mumbling:
'Ho, Tom Bombadil! Where have you come tumbling,
bursting in the front-door? Badger-folk have caught you.
You'll never find it out, the way that we have brought you!'

'Now, old Badger-brock, do you hear me talking?
You show me out at once! I must be a-walking.
Show me to your backdoor under briar-roses;
then clean grimy paws, wipe your earthy noses!
Go back to sleep again on your straw pillow,
like fair Goldberry and Old Man Willow!'

Then all the Badger-folk said: 'We beg your pardon!'
They showed Tom out again to their thorny garden,
went back and hid themselves, a-shivering and a-shaking,
blocked up all their doors, earth together raking.

Rain had passed. The sky was clear, and in the summer-
                                              gloaming
Old Tom Bombadil laughed as he came homing,
unlocked his door again, and opened up a shutter.
In the kitchen round the lamp moths began to flutter;
Tom through the window saw waking stars come winking,
and the new slender moon early westward sinking.

Dark came under Hill. Tom, he lit a candle;
upstairs creaking went, turned the door-handle.
'Hoo, Tom Bombadil! Look what night has brought you!
I'm here behind the door. Now at last I've caught you!
You'd forgotten Barrow-wight dwelling in the old mound
up there on hill-top with the ring of stones round.
He's got loose again. Under earth he'll take you.
Poor Tom Bombadil, pale and cold he'll make you!'

'Go out! Shut the door, and never come back after!
Take away gleaming eyes, take your hollow laughter!
Go back to grassy mound, on your stony pillow
lay down your bony head, like Old Man Willow,

13

like young Goldberry, and Badger-folk in burrow!
Go back to buried gold and forgotten sorrow!'

Out fled Barrow-wight through the window leaping,
through the yard, over wall like a shadow sweeping,
up hill wailing went back to leaning stone-rings,
back under lonely mound, rattling his bone-rings.

Old Tom Bombadil lay upon his pillow
sweeter than Goldberry, quieter than the Willow,
snugger than the Badger-folk or the Barrow-dwellers;
slept like a humming-top, snored like a bellows.

He woke in morning-light, whistled like a starling,
sang, 'Come, derry-dol, merry-dol, my darling!'
He clapped on his battered hat, boots, and coat and feather;
opened the window wide to the sunny weather.

Wise old Bombadil, he was a wary fellow;
bright blue his jacket was, and his boots were yellow.
None ever caught old Tom in upland or in dingle,
walking the forest-paths, or by the Withywindle,
or out on the lily-pools in boat upon the water.
But one day Tom, he went and caught the River-daughter,
in green gown, flowing hair, sitting in the rushes,
singing old water-songs to birds upon the bushes.

He caught her, held her fast! Water-rats went scuttering
reeds hissed, herons cried, and her heart was fluttering.
Said Tom Bombadil: 'Here's my pretty maiden!
You shall come home with me! The table is all laden:
yellow cream, honeycomb, white bread and butter;
roses at the window-sill and peeping round the shutter.
You shall come under Hill! Never mind your mother
in her deep weedy pool: there you'll find no lover!'

Old Tom Bombadil had a merry wedding,
crowned all with buttercups, hat and feather shedding;
his bride with forgetmenots and flag-lilies for garland
was robed all in silver-green. He sang like a starling,
hummed like a honey-bee, lilted to the fiddle,
clasping his river-maid round her slender middle.

Lamps gleamed within his house, and white was the bedding;
in the bright honey-moon Badger-folk came treading,
danced down under Hill, and Old Man Willow
tapped, tapped at window-pane, as they slept on the pillow,
on the bank in the reeds River-woman sighing
heard old Barrow-wight in his mound crying.

Old Tom Bombadil heeded not the voices,
taps, knocks, dancing feet, all the nightly noises;
slept till the sun arose, then sang like a starling:
'Hey! Come derry-dol, merry-dol, my darling!'
sitting on the door-step chopping sticks of willow,
while fair Goldberry combed her tresses yellow.

# 2

# BOMBADIL GOES BOATING

The old year was turning brown; the West Wind was calling;
Tom caught a beechen leaf in the Forest falling.
'I've caught a happy day blown me by the breezes!
Why wait till morrow-year? I'll take it when me pleases.
This day I'll mend my boat and journey as it chances
west down the withy-stream, following my fancies!'

Little Bird sat on twig. 'Whillo, Tom! I heed you.
I've a guess, I've a guess where your fancies lead you.
Shall I go, shall I go, bring him word to meet you?'

'No names, you tell-tale, or I'll skin and eat you,
babbling in every ear things that don't concern you!
If you tell Willow-man where I've gone, I'll burn you,
roast you on a willow-spit. That'll end your prying!'

Willow-wren cocked her tail, piped as she went flying:
'Catch me first, catch me first! No names are needed.
I'll perch on his hither ear: the message will be heeded.
"Down by Mithe", I'll say, "just as sun is sinking"
Hurry up, hurry up! That's the time for drinking!'

Tom laughed to himself: 'Maybe then I'll go there.
I might go by other ways, but today I'll row there.'
He shaved oars, patched his boat; from hidden creek he
                                                    hauled her
through reed and sallow-brake, under leaning alder,
then down the river went, singing: 'Silly-sallow,
Flow withy-willow-stream over deep and shallow!'

'Whee! Tom Bombadil! Whither be you going,
bobbing in a cockle-boat, down the river rowing?'

'Maybe to Brandywine along the Withywindle;
maybe friends of mine fire for me will kindle
down by the Hays-end. Little folk I know there,
kind at the day's end. Now and then I go there'.

'Take word to my kin, bring me back their tidings!
Tell me of diving pools and the fishes' hidings!'

'Nay then', said Bombadil, 'I am only rowing
just to smell the water like, not on errands going'.

'Tee hee! Cocky Tom! Mind your tub don't founder!
Look out for willow-snags! I'd laugh to see you flounder'.

'Talk less, Fisher Blue! Keep your kindly wishes!
Fly off and preen yourself with the bones of fishes!
Gay lord on your bough, at home a dirty varlet
living in a sloven house, though your breast be scarlet.
I've heard of fisher-birds beak in air a-dangling
to show how the wind is set: that's an end of angling!'

The King's fisher shut his beak, winked his eye, as singing
Tom passed under bough. Flash! then he went winging;
dropped down jewel-blue a feather, and Tom caught it
gleaming in a sun-ray: a pretty gift he thought it.
He stuck it in his tall hat, the old feather casting:
'Blue now for Tom', he said, 'a merry hue and lasting!'

Rings swirled round his boat, he saw the bubbles quiver.
Tom slapped his oar, smack! at a shadow in the river.
'Hoosh! Tom Bombadil! 'Tis long since last I met you.
Turned water-boatman, eh? What if I upset you?'

'What? Why, Whisker-lad, I'd ride you down the river.
My fingers on your back would set your hide a-shiver.'

'Pish, Tom Bombadil! I'll go and tell my mother;
"Call all our kin to come, father, sister, brother!
Tom's gone mad as a coot with wooden legs: he's paddling
down Withywindle stream, an old tub a-straddling!"'

'I'll give your otter-fell to Barrow-wights. They'll taw you!
Then smother you in gold-rings! Your mother if she saw you,
she'd never know her son, unless 'twas by a whisker.
Nay, don't tease old Tom, until you be far brisker!'

'Whoosh! said otter-lad, river-water spraying
over Tom's hat and all; set the boat a-swaying,
dived down under it, and by the bank lay peering,
till Tom's merry song faded out of hearing.

Old Swan of Elvet-isle sailed past him proudly,
gave Tom a black look, snorted at him loudly.
Tom laughed: 'You old cob, do you miss your feather?
Give me a new one then! The old was worn by weather.
Could you speak a fair word, I would love you dearer:
long neck and dumb throat, but still a haughty sneerer!
If one day the King returns, in upping he may take you,
brand your yellow bill, and less lordly make you!'
Old Swan huffed his wings, hissed, and paddled faster;
in his wake bobbing on Tom went rowing after.

Tom came to Withy-weir. Down the river rushing
foamed into Windle-reach, a-bubbling and a-splashing;
bore Tom over stone spinning like a windfall,
bobbing like a bottle-cork, to the hythe at Grindwall.

'Hoy! Here's Woodman Tom with his billy-beard on!'
laughed all the little folk of Hays-end and Breredon.
'Ware, Tom! We'll shoot you dead with our bows and arrows!
We don't let Forest-folk nor bogies from the Barrows
cross over Brandywine by cockle-boat nor ferry'.
'Fie, little fatbellies! Don't ye make so merry!

I've seen hobbit-folk digging holes to hide 'em,
frightened if a horny goat or a badger eyed 'em,
afeared of the moony-beams, their own shadows shunning.
I'll call the orks on you: that'll send you running!'

'You may call, Woodman Tom. And you can talk your
                                                beard off.
Three arrows in your hat! You we're not afeared of!
Where would you go to now? If for beer you're making,
the barrels aint deep enough in Breredon for your slaking!'

'Away over Brandywine by Shirebourn I'd be going,
but too swift for cockle-boat the river now is flowing.
I'd bless little folk that took me in their wherry,
wish them evenings fair and many mornings merry'.

Red flowed the Brandywine; with flame the river kindled,
as sun sank beyond the Shire, and then to grey it dwindled.
Mithe Steps empty stood. None was there to greet him.
Silent the Causeway lay. Said Tom: 'A merry meeting!'

Tom stumped along the road, as the light was failing.
Rushey lamps gleamed ahead. He heard a voice him hailing.
'Whoa there!' Ponies stopped, wheels halted sliding.
Tom went plodding past, never looked beside him.

'Ho there! beggarman tramping in the Marish!
What's your business here? Hat all stuck with arrows!
Someone's warned you off, caught you at your sneaking?
Come here! Tell me now what it is you're seeking!
Shire-ale, I'll be bound, though you've not a penny.
I'll bid them lock their doors, and then you won't get any!'

'Well, well, Muddy-feet! From one that's late for meeting
away back by the Mithe that's a surly greeting!
You old farmer fat that cannot walk for wheezing,
cart-drawn like a sack, ought to be more pleasing.

Penny-wise tub-on-legs! A beggar can't be chooser,
or else I'd bid you go, and you would be the loser.
Come, Maggot! Help me up! A tankard now you owe me.
Even in cockshut light an old friend should know me!'

Laughing they drove away, in Rushey never halting,
though the inn open stood and they could smell the malting.
They turned down Maggot's Lane, rattling and bumping,
Tom in the farmer's cart dancing round and jumping.
Stars shone on Bamfurlong, and Maggot's house was lighted;
fire in the kitchen burned to welcome the benighted.

Maggot's sons bowed at door, his daughters did their curtsy,
his wife brought tankards out for those that might be thirsty.
Songs they had and merry tales, the supping and the dancing;
Goodman Maggot there for all his belt was prancing,
Tom did a hornpipe when he was not quaffing,
daughters did the Springle-ring, goodwife did the laughing.

When others went to bed in hay, fern, or feather,
close in the inglenook they laid their heads together,
old Tom and Muddy-feet, swapping all the tidings
from Barrow-downs to Tower Hills: of walkings and of
                                                    ridings;
of wheat-ear and barley-corn, of sowing and of reaping;
queer tales from Bree, and talk at smithy, mill, and cheaping;
rumours in whispering trees, south-wind in the larches,
tall Watchers by the Ford, Shadows on the marches.

Old Maggot slept at last in chair beside the embers.
Ere dawn Tom was gone: as dreams one half remembers,
some merry, some sad, and some of hidden warning.
None heard the door unlocked; a shower of rain at morning
his footprints washed away, at Mithe he left no traces,
at Hays-end they heard no song nor sound of heavy paces.

Three days his boat lay by the hythe at Grindwall,
and then one morn was gone back up Withywindle.
Otter-folk, hobbits said, came by night and loosed her,
dragged her over weir, and up stream they pushed her.

Out from Elvet-isle Old Swan came sailing,
in beak took her painter up in the water trailing,
drew her proudly on; otters swam beside her
round old Willow-man's crooked roots to guide her;
the King's fisher perched on bow, on thwart the wren was
singing,
merrily the cockle-boat homeward they were bringing.
To Tom's creek they came at last. Otter-lad said: 'Whish now!
What's a coot without his legs, or a finless fish now?'
O! silly-sallow-willow-stream! The oars they'd left behind
them!
Long they lay at Grindwall hythe for Tom to come and find
them.

# 3

# ERRANTRY

There was a merry passenger,
a messenger, a mariner:
he built a gilded gondola
to wander in, and had in her
a load of yellow oranges
and porridge for his provender;
he perfumed her with marjoram
and cardamom and lavender.

He called the winds of argosies
with cargoes in to carry him
across the rivers seventeen
that lay between to tarry him.
He landed all in loneliness
where stonily the pebbles on
the running river Derrilyn
goes merrily for ever on.
He journeyed then through meadow-lands
to Shadow-land that dreary lay,
and under hill and over hill
went roving still a weary way.

He sat and sang a melody,
his errantry a-tarrying;
he begged a pretty butterfly
that fluttered by to marry him.
She scorned him and she scoffed at him,
she laughed at him unpitying;
so long he studied wizardry
and sigaldry and smithying.

He wove a tissue airy-thin
to snare her in; to follow her
he made him beetle-leather wing
and feather wing of swallow-hair.
He caught her in bewilderment
with filament of spider-thread;
he made her soft pavilions
of lilies, and a bridal bed
of flowers and of thistle-down
to nestle down and rest her in;
and silken webs of filmy white
and silver light he dressed her in.

He threaded gems in necklaces,
but recklessly she squandered them
and fell to bitter quarrelling;
then sorrowing he wandered on,
and there he left her withering,
as shivering he fled away;
with windy weather following
on swallow-wing he sped away.

He passed the archipelagoes
where yellow grows the marigold,
where countless silver fountains are,
and mountains are of fairy-gold.
He took to war and foraying,
a-harrying beyond the sea,
and roaming over Belmarie
and Thellamie and Fantasie.

He made a shield and morion
of coral and of ivory,
a sword he made of emerald,
and terrible his rivalry
with elven-knights of Aerie
and Faerie, with paladins

that golden-haired and shining-eyed
came riding by and challenged him.

Of crystal was his habergeon,
his scabbard of chalcedony;
with silver tipped at plenilune
his spear was hewn of ebony.
His javelins were of malachite
and stalactite—he brandished them,
and went and fought the dragon-flies
of Paradise, and vanquished them.

He battled with the Dumbledors,
the Hummerhorns, and Honeybees,
and won the Golden Honeycomb;
and running home on sunny seas
in ship of leaves and gossamer
with blossom for a canopy,
he sat and sang, and furbished up
and burnished up his panoply.

He tarried for a little while
in little isles that lonely lay,
and found there naught but blowing grass;
and so at last the only way
he took, and turned, and coming home
with honeycomb, to memory
his message came, and errand too!
In derring-do and glamoury
he had forgot them, journeying
and tourneying, a wanderer.
So now he must depart again
and start again his gondola,
for ever still a messenger,
a passenger, a tarrier,
a-roving as a feather does,
a weather-driven mariner.

# 4

# PRINCESS MEE

Little Princess Mee
Lovely was she
As in elven-song is told:
  She had pearls in hair
  All threaded fair;
Of gossamer shot with gold
  Was her kerchief made,
  And a silver braid
Of stars about her throat.
  Of moth-web light
  All moonlit-white
She wore a woven coat,
  And round her kirtle
  Was bound a girdle
Sewn with diamond dew.

  She walked by day
  Under mantle grey
And hood of clouded blue;
  But she went by night
  All glittering bright
Under the starlit sky,
  And her slippers frail
  Of fishes' mail
Flashed as she went by
  To her dancing-pool,
  And on mirror cool
Of windless water played.
  As a mist of light
  In whirling flight

A glint like glass she made
　　Wherever her feet
　　Of silver fleet
Flicked the dancing-floor.

　　She looked on high
　　To the roofless sky,
And she looked to the shadowy shore;
　　Then round she went,
　　And her eyes she bent
And saw beneath her go
　　A Princess Shee
　　As fair as Mee:
They were dancing toe to toe!

　　Shee was as light
　　As Mee, and as bright;
But Shee was, strange to tell,
　　Hanging down
　　With starry crown
Into a bottomless well!
　　Her gleaming eyes
　　In great surprise
Looked up to the eyes of Mee:
　　A marvellous thing,
　　Head-down to swing
Above a starry sea!

　　Only their feet
　　Could ever meet;
For where the ways might lie
　　To find a land
　　Where they do not stand
But hang down in the sky
　　No one could tell
　　Nor learn in spell
In all the elven-lore.

So still on her own
An elf alone
Dancing as before
With pearls in hair
And kirtle fair
And slippers frail
Of fishes' mail went Mee:
Of fishes' mail
And slippers frail
And kirtle fair
With pearls in hair went Shee!

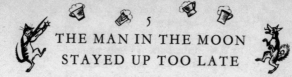

# 5

# THE MAN IN THE MOON
## STAYED UP TOO LATE

There is an inn, a merry old inn
  beneath an old grey hill,
And there they brew a beer so brown
That the Man in the Moon himself came down
  one night to drink his fill.

The ostler has a tipsy cat
  that plays a five-stringed fiddle;
And up and down he runs his bow,
Now squeaking high, now purring low,
  now sawing in the middle.

The landlord keeps a little dog
  that is mighty fond of jokes;
When there's good cheer among the guests,
He cocks an ear at all the jests
  and laughs until he chokes.

They also keep a hornéd cow
  as proud as any queen;
But music turns her head like ale,
And makes her wave her tufted tail
  and dance upon the green.

And O! the row of silver dishes
  and the store of silver spoons!
For Sunday there's a special pair,
And these they polish up with care
  on Saturday afternoons.

31

The Man in the Moon was drinking deep,
    and the cat began to wail;
A dish and a spoon on the table danced,
The cow in the garden madly pranced,
    and the little dog chased his tail.

The Man in the Moon took another mug,
    and then rolled beneath his chair;
And there he dozed and dreamed of ale,
Till in the sky the stars were pale,
    and dawn was in the air.

The ostler said to his tipsy cat:
    'The white horses of the Moon,
They neigh and champ their silver bits;
But their master's been and drowned his wits,
    and the Sun'll be rising soon!'

So the cat on his fiddle played hey-diddle-diddle,
    a jig that would wake the dead:
He squeaked and sawed and quickened the tune,
While the landlord shook the Man in the Moon:
    'It's after three!' he said.

They rolled the Man slowly up the hill
    and bundled him into the Moon,
While his horses galloped up in rear,
And the cow came capering like a deer,
    and a dish ran up with a spoon.

Now quicker the fiddle went deedle-dum-diddle;
    the dog began to roar,
The cow and the horses stood on their heads;
The guests all bounded from their beds
    and danced upon the floor.

With a ping and a pong the fiddle-strings broke!
    the cow jumped over the Moon,

And the little dog laughed to see such fun,
And the Saturday dish went off at a run
  with the silver Sunday spoon.

The round Moon rolled behind the hill,
  as the Sun raised up her head.
She hardly believed her fiery eyes;
For though it was day, to her surprise
  they all went back to bed!

# 6

# THE MAN IN THE MOON
# CAME DOWN TOO SOON

The Man in the Moon had silver shoon,
  and his beard was of silver thread;
With opals crowned and pearls all bound
  about his girdlestead,
In his mantle grey he walked one day
  across a shining floor,
And with crystal key in secrecy
  he opened an ivory door.

On a filigree stair of glimmering hair
  then lightly down he went,
And merry was he at last to be free
  on a mad adventure bent.
In diamonds white he had lost delight;
  he was tired of his minaret
Of tall moonstone that towered alone
  on a lunar mountain set.

He would dare any peril for ruby and beryl
  to broider his pale attire,
For new diadems of lustrous gems,
  emerald and sapphire.
He was lonely too with nothing to do
  but stare at the world of gold
And heark to the hum that would distantly come
  as gaily round it rolled.

34

At plenilune in his argent moon
    in his heart he longed for Fire:
Not the limpid lights of wan selenites;
    for red was his desire,
For crimson and rose and ember-glows,
    for flame with burning tongue,
For the scarlet skies in a swift sunrise
    when a stormy day is young.

He'd have seas of blues, and the living hues
    of forest green and fen;
And he yearned for the mirth of the populous earth
    and the sanguine blood of men.
He coveted song, and laughter long,
    and viands hot, and wine,
Eating pearly cakes of light snowflakes
    and drinking thin moonshine.

He twinkled his feet, as he thought of the meat,
    of pepper, and punch galore;
And he tripped unaware on his slanting stair,
    and like a meteor,
A star in flight, ere Yule one night
    flickering down he fell
From his laddery path to a foaming bath
    in the windy Bay of Bel.

He began to think, lest he melt and sink,
    what in the moon to do,
When a fisherman's boat found him far afloat
    to the amazement of the crew,
Caught in their net all shimmering wet
    in a phosphorescent sheen
Of bluey whites and opal lights
    and delicate liquid green.

Against his wish with the morning fish
    they packed him back to land:

'You had best get a bed in an inn', they said;
  'the town is near at hand'.
Only the knell of one slow bell
  high in the Seaward Tower
Announced the news of his moonsick cruise
  at that unseemly hour.

Not a hearth was laid, not a breakfast made,
  and dawn was cold and damp.
There were ashes for fire, and for grass the mire,
  for the sun a smoking lamp
In a dim back-street. Not a man did he meet,
  no voice was raised in song;
There were snores instead, for all folk were abed
  and still would slumber long.

He knocked as he passed on doors locked fast,
  and called and cried in vain,
Till he came to an inn that had light within,
  and tapped at a window-pane.
A drowsy cook gave a surly look,
  and 'What do you want?' said he.
'I want fire and gold and songs of old
  and red wine flowing free!'

'You won't get them here', said the cook with a leer,
  'but you may come inside.
Silver I lack and silk to my back—
  maybe I'll let you bide'.
A silver gift the latch to lift,
  a pearl to pass the door;
For a seat by the cook in the ingle-nook
  it cost him twenty more.

For hunger or drouth naught passed his mouth
  till he gave both crown and cloak;
And all that he got, in an earthen pot
  broken and black with smoke,

Was porridge cold and two days old
    to eat with a wooden spoon.
For puddings of Yule with plums, poor fool,
    he arrived so much too soon:
An unwary guest on a lunatic quest
    from the Mountains of the Moon.

# 7

# THE STONE TROLL

Troll sat alone on his seat of stone,
And munched and mumbled a bare old bone;
   For many a year he had gnawed it near,
     For meat was hard to come by.
       Done by! Gum by!
   In a cave in the hills he dwelt alone,
     And meat was hard to come by.

Up came Tom with his big boots on.
Said he to Troll: 'Pray, what is yon?
   For it looks like the shin o' my nuncle Tim,
     As should be a-lyin' in graveyard.
       Caveyard! Paveyard!
   This many a year has Tim been gone,
     And I thought he were lyin' in graveyard'.

'My lad', said Troll, 'this bone I stole.
But what be bones that lie in a hole?
   Thy nuncle was dead as a lump o' lead,
     Afore I found his shinbone.
       Tinbone! Thinbone!
   He can spare a share for a poor old troll;
     For he don't need his shinbone'.

Said Tom: 'I don't see why the likes o' thee
Without axin' leave should go makin' free
   With the shank or the shin o' my father's kin;
     So hand the old bone over!
       Rover! Trover!
   Though dead he be, it belongs to he;
     So hand the old bone over!'

'For a couple o' pins', says Troll, and grins,
'I'll eat thee too, and gnaw thy shins.
   A bit o' fresh meat will go down sweet!
      I'll try my teeth on thee now.
         Hee now! See now!
   I'm tired o' gnawing old bones and skins;
      I've a mind to dine on thee now'.


But just as he thought his dinner was caught,
He found his hands had hold of naught.
   Before he could mind, Tom slipped behind
      And gave him the boot to larn him.
         Warn him! Darn him!
   A bump o' the boot on the seat, Tom thought,
      Would be the way to larn him.


But harder than stone is the flesh and bone
Of a troll that sits in the hills alone.
   As well set your boot to the mountain's root,
      For the seat of a troll don't feel it.
         Peel it! Heal it!
   Old Troll laughed, when he heard Tom groan,
      And he knew his toes could feel it.


Tom's leg is game, since home he came,
And his bootless foot is lasting lame;
   But Troll don't care, and he's still there
      With the bone he boned from its owner.
         Doner! Boner!
   Troll's old seat is still the same,
      And the bone he boned from its owner!

# 8

# PERRY-THE-WINKLE

The Lonely Troll he sat on a stone
   and sang a mournful lay:
'O why, O why must I live on my own
   in the hills of Faraway?
My folk are gone beyond recall
   and take no thought of me;
alone I'm left, the last of all
   from Weathertop to the Sea'.

'I steal no gold, I drink no beer,
   I eat no kind of meat;
but People slam their doors in fear,
   whenever they hear my feet.
O how I wish that they were neat,
   and my hands were not so rough!
Yet my heart is soft, my smile is sweet,
   and my cooking good enough.'

'Come, come!' he thought, 'this will not do!
   I must go and find a friend;
a-walking soft I'll wander through
   the Shire from end to end'.
Down he went, and he walked all night
   with his feet in boots of fur;
to Delving he came in the morning light,
   when folk were just astir.

He looked around, and who did he meet
   but old Mrs. Bunce and all
with umbrella and basket walking the street;
   and he smiled and stopped to call:

'Good morning, ma'am! Good day to you!
   I hope I find you well?'
But she dropped umbrella and basket too,
   and yelled a frightful yell.

Old Pott the Mayor was strolling near;
   when he heard that awful sound,
he turned all purple and pink with fear,
   and dived down underground.
The Lonely Troll was hurt and sad:
   'Don't go!' he gently said,
but old Mrs. Bunce ran home like mad
   and hid beneath her bed.

The Troll went on to the market-place
   and peeped above the stalls;
the sheep went wild when they saw his face,
   and the geese flew over the walls.
Old Farmer Hogg he spilled his ale,
   Bill Butcher threw a knife,
and Grip his dog, he turned his tail
   and ran to save his life.

The old Troll sadly sat and wept
   outside the Lockholes gate,
and Perry-the-Winkle up he crept
   and patted him on the pate.
'O why do you weep, you great big lump?
   You're better outside than in!'
He gave the Troll a friendly thump,
   and laughed to see him grin.

'O Perry-the-Winkle boy', he cried,
   'come, you're the lad for me!
Now if you're willing to take a ride,
   I'll carry you home to tea'.

He jumped on his back and held on tight,
    and 'Off you go!' said he;
and the Winkle had a feast that night,
    and sat on the old Troll's knee.

There were pikelets, there was buttered toast,
    and jam, and cream, and cake,
and the Winkle strove to eat the most,
    though his buttons all should break.
The kettle sang, the fire was hot,
    the pot was large and brown,
and the Winkle tried to drink the lot,
    in tea though he should drown.

When full and tight were coat and skin,
    they rested without speech,
till the old Troll said: 'I'll now begin
    the baker's art to teach,
the making of beautiful cramsome bread,
    of bannocks light and brown;
and then you can sleep on a heather-bed
    with pillows of owlets' down'.

'Young Winkle, where've you been?' they said.
    'I've been to a fulsome tea,
and I feel so fat, for I have fed
    on cramsome bread', said he.
'But where, my lad, in the Shire was that?
    Or out in Bree?' said they.
But Winkle he up and answered flat:
    'I aint a-going to say'.

'But I know where', said Peeping Jack,
    'I watched him ride away:
he went upon the old Troll's back
    to the hills of Faraway'.
Then all the People went with a will,

by pony, cart, or moke,
until they came to a house in a hill
and saw a chimney smoke.

They hammered upon the old Troll's door.
'A beautiful cramsome cake
O bake for us, please, or two, or more;
O bake!' they cried, 'O bake!'
'Go home, go home!' the old Troll said.
'I never invited you.
Only on Thursdays I bake my bread,
and only for a few'.

'Go home! Go home! There's some mistake.
My house is far too small;
and I've no pikelets, cream, or cake:
the Winkle has eaten all!
You Jack, and Hogg, old Bunce and Pott
I wish no more to see.
Be off! Be off now all the lot!
The Winkle's the boy for me!'

Now Perry-the-Winkle grew so fat
through eating of cramsome bread,
his weskit bust, and never a hat
would sit upon his head;
for Every Thursday he went to tea,
and sat on the kitchen floor,
and smaller the old Troll seemed to be,
as he grew more and more.

The Winkle a Baker great became,
as still is said in song;
from the Sea to Bree there went the fame
of his bread both short and long.
But it weren't so good as the cramsome bread;
no butter so rich and free,
as Every Thursday the old Troll spread
for Perry-the-Winkle's tea.

# 9

# THE MEWLIPS

The shadows where the Mewlips dwell
   Are dark and wet as ink,
And slow and softly rings their bell,
   As in the slime you sink.

You sink into the slime, who dare
   To knock upon their door,
While down the grinning gargoyles stare
   And noisome waters pour.

Beside the rotting river-strand
   The drooping willows weep,
And gloomily the gorcrows stand
   Croaking in their sleep.

Over the Merlock Mountains a long and weary way,
  In a mouldy valley where the trees are grey,
By a dark pool's borders without wind or tide,
  Moonless and sunless, the Mewlips hide.

The cellars where the Mewlips sit
   Are deep and dank and cold
With single sickly candle lit;
   And there they count their gold.

Their walls are wet, their ceilings drip;
   Their feet upon the floor
Go softly with a squish-flap-flip,
   As they sidle to the door.

They peep out slyly; through a crack
Their feeling fingers creep,
And when they've finished, in a sack
Your bones they take to keep.

Beyond the Merlock Mountains, a long and lonely road,
Through the spider-shadows and the marsh of Tode,
And through the wood of hanging trees and the gallows-
weed,
You go to find the Mewlips—and the Mewlips feed.

# 10

# OLIPHAUNT

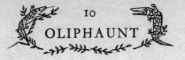

Grey as a mouse,
Big as a house,
Nose like a snake,
I make the earth shake,
As I tramp through the grass;
Trees crack as I pass.
With horns in my mouth
I walk in the South,
Flapping big ears.
Beyond count of years
I stump round and round,
Never lie on the ground,
Not even to die.
Oliphaunt am I,
Biggest of all,
Huge, old, and tall.
If ever you'd met me,
You wouldn't forget me.
If you never do,
You won't think I'm true;
But old Oliphaunt am I,
And I never lie.

# II
# FASTITOCALON

Look, there is Fastitocalon!
An island good to land upon,
   Although 'tis rather bare.
Come, leave the sea! And let us run,
Or dance, or lie down in the sun!
    See, gulls are sitting there!
      Beware!
     Gulls do not sink.
There they may sit, or strut and prink:
Their part it is to tip the wink,
   If anyone should dare
   Upon that isle to settle,
Or only for a while to get
Relief from sickness or the wet,
   Or maybe boil a kettle.

Ah! foolish folk, who land on HIM,
And little fires proceed to trim
   And hope perhaps for tea!
It may be that His shell is thick,
He seems to sleep; but He is quick,
    And floats now in the sea
      With guile;
And when He hears their tapping feet,
Or faintly feels the sudden heat,
      With smile
      HE dives,
And promptly turning upside-down
He tips them off, and deep they drown,
    And lose their silly lives
      To their surprise.

Be wise!
There are many monsters in the Sea,
But none so perilous as HE,
Old horny Fastitocalon,
Whose mighty kindred all have gone,
The last of the old Turtle-fish.
So if to save your life you wish
  Then I advise:
Pay heed to sailors' ancient lore,
Set foot on no uncharted shore!
  Or better still,
Your days at peace on Middle-earth
   In mirth
   Fulfill!

# CAT

The fat cat on the mat
    may seem to dream
of nice mice that suffice
    for him, or cream;
but he free, maybe,
    walks in thought
unbowed, proud, where loud
    roared and fought
his kin, lean and slim,
    or deep in den
in the East feasted on beasts
    and tender men.

The giant lion with iron
    claw in paw,
and huge ruthless tooth
    in gory jaw;
the pard dark-starred,
    fleet upon feet,
that oft soft from aloft
    leaps on his meat
where woods loom in gloom—
    far now they be,
    fierce and free,
    and tamed is he;
but fat cat on the mat
    kept as a pet,
    he does not forget.

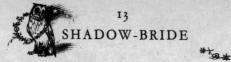

# SHADOW-BRIDE

There was a man who dwelt alone,
    as day and night went past
he sat as still as carven stone,
    and yet no shadow cast.
The white owls perched upon his head
    beneath the winter moon;
they wiped their beaks and thought him dead
    under the stars of June.

There came a lady clad in grey
    in the twilight shining:
one moment she would stand and stay,
    her hair with flowers entwining.
He woke, as had he sprung of stone,
    and broke the spell that bound him;
he clasped her fast, both flesh and bone,
    and wrapped her shadow round him.

There never more she walks her ways
    by sun or moon or star;
she dwells below where neither days
    nor any nights there are.
But once a year when caverns yawn
    and hidden things awake,
they dance together then till dawn
    and a single shadow make.

# THE HOARD

When the moon was new and the sun young
of silver and gold the gods sung:
in the green grass they silver spilled,
and the white waters they with gold filled.
Ere the pit was dug or Hell yawned,
ere dwarf was bred or dragon spawned,
there were Elves of old, and strong spells
under green hills in hollow dells
they sang as they wrought many fair things,
and the bright crowns of the Elf-kings.
But their doom fell, and their song waned,
by iron hewn and by steel chained.
Greed that sang not, nor with mouth smiled,
in dark holes their wealth piled,
graven silver and carven gold:
over Elvenhome the shadow rolled.

There was an old dwarf in a dark cave,
to silver and gold his fingers clave;
with hammer and tongs and anvil-stone
he worked his hands to the hard bone,
and coins he made, and strings of rings,
and thought to buy the power of kings.
But his eyes grew dim and his ears dull
and the skin yellow on his old skull;
through his bony claw with a pale sheen
the stony jewels slipped unseen.
No feet he heard, though the earth quaked,
when the young dragon his thirst slaked,

and the stream smoked at his dark door.
The flames hissed on the dank floor.
and he died alone in the red fire;
his bones were ashes in the hot mire.

There was an old dragon under grey stone;
his red eyes blinked as he lay alone.
His joy was dead and his youth spent,
he was knobbed and wrinkled, and his limbs bent
in the long years to his gold chained;
in his heart's furnace the fire waned.
To his belly's slime gems stuck thick,
silver and gold he would snuff and lick:
he knew the place of the least ring
beneath the shadow of his black wing.
Of thieves he thought on his hard bed,
and dreamed that on their flesh he fed,
their bones crushed, and their blood drank:
his ears drooped and his breath sank.
Mail-rings rang. He heard them not.
A voice echoed in his deep grot:
a young warrior with a bright sword
called him forth to defend his hoard.
His teeth were knives, and of horn his hide,
but iron tore him, and his flame died.

There was an old king on a high throne:
his white beard lay on knees of bone;
his mouth savoured neither meat nor drink,
nor his ears song; he could only think
of his huge chest with carven lid
where pale gems and gold lay hid
in secret treasury in the dark ground;
its strong doors were iron-bound.
The swords of his thanes were dull with rust,
his glory fallen, his rule unjust,
his halls hollow, and his bowers cold,
but king he was of elvish gold.

He heard not the horns in the mountain-pass,
he smelt not the blood on the trodden grass,
but his halls were burned, his kingdom lost;
in a cold pit his bones were tossed.

There is an old hoard in a dark rock,
forgotten behind doors none can unlock;
that grim gate no man can pass.
On the mound grows the green grass;
there sheep feed and the larks soar,
and the wind blows from the sea-shore.
The old hoard the Night shall keep,
while earth waits and the Elves sleep.

# 15
# THE SEA-BELL

I walked by the sea, and there came to me,
    as a star-beam on the wet sand,
a white shell like a sea-bell;
    trembling it lay in my wet hand.
In my fingers shaken I heard waken
    a ding within, by a harbour bar
a buoy swinging, a call ringing
    over endless seas, faint now and far.

Then I saw a boat silently float
    on the night-tide, empty and grey.
'It is later than late! Why do we wait?'
    I leapt in and cried: 'Bear me away!'

It bore me away, wetted with spray,
    wrapped in a mist, wound in a sleep,
to a forgotten strand in a strange land.
    In the twilight beyond the deep
I heard a sea-bell swing in the swell,
    dinging, dinging, and the breakers roar
on the hidden teeth of a perilous reef;
    and at last I came to a long shore.
White it glimmered, and the sea simmered
    with star-mirrors in a silver net;
cliffs of stone pale as ruel-bone
    in the moon-foam were gleaming wet.
Glittering sand slid through my hand,
    dust of pearl and jewel-grist,
trumpets of opal, roses of coral,
    flutes of green and amethyst.

But under cliff-eaves there were glooming caves,
    weed-curtained, dark and grey;
a cold air stirred in my hair,
    and the light waned, as I hurried away.

Down from a hill ran a green rill;
    its water I drank to my heart's ease.
Up its fountain-stair to a country fair
    of ever-eve I came, far from the seas,
climbing into meadows of fluttering shadows:
    flowers lay there like fallen stars,
and on a blue pool, glassy and cool,
    like floating moons the nenuphars.
Alders were sleeping, and willows weeping
    by a slow river of rippling weeds;
gladdon-swords guarded the fords,
    and green spears, and arrow-reeds.

There was echo of song all the evening long
    down in the valley; many a thing
running to and fro: hares white as snow,
    voles out of holes; moths on the wing
with lantern-eyes; in quiet surprise
    brocks were staring out of dark doors.
I heard dancing there, music in the air,
    feet going quick on the green floors.
But wherever I came it was ever the same:
    the feet fled, and all was still;
never a greeting, only the fleeting
    pipes, voices, horns on the hill.

Of river-leaves and the rush-sheaves
    I made me a mantle of jewel-green,
a tall wand to hold, and a flag of gold;
    my eyes shone like the star-sheen.
With flowers crowned I stood on a mound,
    and shrill as a call at cock-crow

proudly I cried: 'Why do you hide?
   Why do none speak, wherever I go?
Here now I stand, king of this land,
   with gladdon-sword and reed-mace.
Answer my call! Come forth all!
   Speak to me words! Show me a face!'

Black came a cloud as a night-shroud.
   Like a dark mole groping I went,
to the ground falling, on my hands crawling
   with eyes blind and my back bent.
I crept to a wood: silent it stood
   in its dead leaves; bare were its boughs.
There must I sit, wandering in wit,
   while owls snored in their hollow house.
For a year and a day there must I stay:
   beetles were tapping in the rotten trees,
spiders were weaving, in the mould heaving
   puffballs loomed about my knees.

At last there came light in my long night,
   and I saw my hair hanging grey.
'Bent though I be, I must find the sea!
   I have lost myself, and I know not the way,
but let me be gone!' Then I stumbled on;
   like a hunting bat shadow was over me;
in my ears dinned a withering wind,
   and with ragged briars I tried to cover me.
My hands were torn and my knees worn,
   and years were heavy upon my back,
when the rain in my face took a salt taste,
   and I smelled the smell of sea-wrack.

Birds came sailing, mewing, wailing;
   I heard voices in cold caves,
seals barking, and rocks snarling,
   and in spout-holes the gulping of waves.

Winter came fast; into a mist I passed,
   to land's end my years I bore;
snow was in the air, ice in my hair,
   darkness was lying on the last shore.

There still afloat waited the boat,
   in the tide lifting, its prow tossing.
Weary I lay, as it bore me away,
   the waves climbing, the seas crossing,
passing old hulls clustered with gulls
   and great ships laden with light,
coming to haven, dark as a raven,
   silent as snow, deep in the night.

Houses were shuttered, wind round them muttered,
   roads were empty. I sat by a door,
and where drizzling rain poured down a drain
   I cast away all that I bore:
in my clutching hand some grains of sand,
   and a sea-shell silent and dead.
Never will my ear that bell hear,
   never my feet that shore tread
Never again, as in sad lane,
   in blind alley and in long street
ragged I walk. To myself I talk;
   for still they speak not, men that I meet.

# 16

# THE LAST SHIP

Fíriel looked out at three o'clock:
  the grey night was going;
far away a golden cock
  clear and shrill was crowing.
The trees were dark, and the dawn pale,
  waking birds were cheeping,
a wind moved cool and frail
  through dim leaves creeping.

She watched the gleam at window grow,
  till the long light was shimmering
on land and leaf; on grass below
  grey dew was glimmering.
Over the floor her white feet crept,
  down the stair they twinkled,
through the grass they dancing stepped
  all with dew besprinkled.

Her gown had jewels upon its hem,
  as she ran down to the river,
and leaned upon a willow-stem,
  and watched the water quiver.
A kingfisher plunged down like a stone
  in a blue flash falling,
bending reeds were softly blown,
  lily-leaves were sprawling.

A sudden music to her came,
  as she stood there gleaming
with free hair in the morning's flame
  on her shoulders streaming.

Flutes there were, and harps were wrung,
   and there was sound of singing,
like wind-voices keen and young
   and far bells ringing.

A ship with golden beak and oar
   and timbers white came gliding;
swans went sailing on before,
   her tall prow guiding.
Fair folk out of Elvenland
   in silver-grey were rowing,
and three with crowns she saw there stand
   with bright hair flowing.

With harp in hand they sang their song
   to the slow oars swinging:
'Green is the land, the leaves are long,
   and the birds are singing.
Many a day with dawn of gold
   this earth will lighten,
many a flower will yet unfold,
   ere the cornfields whiten.

'Then whither go ye, boatmen fair,
   down the river gliding?
To twilight and to secret lair
   in the great forest hiding?
To Northern isles and shores of stone
   on strong swans flying,
by cold waves to dwell alone
   with the white gulls crying?'

'Nay!' they answered. 'Far away
   on the last road faring,
leaving western havens grey,
   the seas of shadow daring,

we go back to Elvenhome,
    where the White Tree is growing,
and the Star shines upon the foam
    on the last shore flowing.


'To mortal fields say farewell,
    Middle-earth forsaking!
In Elvenhome a clear bell
    in the high tower is shaking.
Here grass fades and leaves fall,
    and sun and moon wither,
and we have heard the far call
    that bids us journey thither'.


The oars were stayed. They turned aside:
    'Do you hear the call, Earth-maiden?
Fíriel! Fíriel!' they cried.
    'Our ship is not full-laden.
One more only we may bear.
    Come! For your days are speeding.
Come! Earth-maiden elven-fair,
    our last call heeding.'


Fíriel looked from the river-bank,
    one step daring;
then deep in clay her feet sank,
    and she halted staring.
Slowly the elven-ship went by
    whispering through the water:
'I cannot come!' they heard her cry.
    'I was born Earth's daughter!'


No jewels bright her gown bore,
    as she walked back from the meadow
under roof and dark door,
    under the house-shadow.

She donned her smock of russet brown,
   her long hair braided,
and to her work came·stepping down.
   Soon the sunlight faded.

Year still after year flows
   down the Seven Rivers;
cloud passes, sunlight glows,
   reed and willow quivers
at morn and eve, but never more
   westward ships have waded
in mortal waters as before,
   and their song has faded.

**THE END**

# BESTSELLERS.
## By and about
# J.R.R. TOLKIEN.
## Today's best-loved author of fantasy.

**Available at your bookstore or use this coupon.**